Bite-Sized Books

Another Way

A call for a new direction in British foreign and defence policy

Steven McCabe

Roger Schafir

Cover by

Dean Stockton

Published by Bite-Sized Books Ltd 2022

Bite-Sized Books Ltd 8th Floor, 20 St. Andrews Street, London EC4A 3AY, UK

Registered in the UK. Company Registration No: 9395379

ISBN: 978-1-7397261-3-3

To Richard (my dentist)
With thanks,
Regards, Roger.

Contents

Chapter 1

Introduction – A New World Order?

Your first reaction to seeing this book may be that the timing alone makes it forlorn. This is appearing soon after the invasion of Ukraine, which at least gives it topicality, but in the present atmosphere our message won't go down well with most of the commentariat and a lot of public opinion. Yet the issues we address go beyond Ukraine and Putin, in fact beyond Russia and its surroundings, and are issues about western policy towards the entire world since the end of Soviet communism. Most of what follows was written before the latest crisis, but for years the only politicians who would give so much as the time of day to the notions we advocate are the Labour left, briefly in charge of the Labour Party, now spectacularly out again. Old New Labour (a useful oxymoron) is back in control, and no more likely (in fact less likely) than the Conservatives to change the fixed attitudes they learnt years ago about what constitutes electable politics.

However, there is nothing specifically left wing at all about what we advocate, and conservatives could also support it. There has recently been the COP climate conference in Glasgow, where Britain's Conservative government trumpeted its commitment to a leading role in changing the entire economy of the world towards a green alternative – a radical break with everything started by the industrial revolution of two centuries ago. Once it would have seemed amazing that a British government would go in such a direction, and a Conservative government at that, for it was among conservatives that climate change denial had its strongest advocates. If conservatives can change their minds about environmentalism when the grounds to do so become strong enough, they can change their minds about an endlessly interventionist foreign policy which can be summarised, briefly but correctly, as: 'The west now rules.'

It is notoriously hard to interest the public generally about foreign affairs, even issues of peace and war except at acute moments. Yet though the public tends to let the decision makers get on with it abroad, when asked they show unenthusiasm for the more militant aspects of it. When missile strikes were carried out against Syria in 2018 in response to a use of chemical weapons by (almost certainly) the Syrian regime, it had to be done quickly and got over with before home opposition got support in the opinion polls. When in the 2017 election the then Labour leader Jeremy Corbyn said that foreign interventions only made things worse, opponents whose mouths moved more quickly than their minds seized the chance to stress that he was soft on defence – if not indeed on the side of Britain's enemies. But within hours Sky News was reporting that they had carried out street interviews in a marginal constituency and couldn't find a single person who disagreed with what Jeremy Corbyn had said. The mainstream politicians persist in their outlook, but the population hang back.

Aftermath of an airstrike on Syria (Source: Syrian civil defence service[1])

Attitudes towards Britain's role abroad come from history of course. After endless wars in previous centuries, Britain ended up in the 19th century as the most powerful country in the world, and possessor of the largest empire in history. Memory of this, and knowledge of its loss, is deep in British thinking. Everyone agrees that Britain's position is not now what it was then, but for many years now there have been a range of views about what should replace it. Here is a summary of what we think the main ones are:

---

[1] Aftermath of an airstrike on the village of Zardana in Syria's Idlib province on 7th June 2018 published in The Independent 8th June 2018 (https://www.independent.co.uk/news/world/middle-east/syria-airstrike-assad-russia-rebel-held-village-idlib-zardata-death-toll-a8388956.html)

- Britain is still a great power and should pursue independent (and armed) policies towards the rest of the world.

  This you could call the old-fashioned right-wing view. Not many people pursue that on its own but also call for Britain maintaining a network of alliances, as in the next option.

- Britain, though certainly staying well armed, should put all its emphasis on alliances with the like-minded, and in particular with the United States.

  This is the orthodox attitude of the mainstream politicians.

- Britain should be well armed and in military alliances, but these should be multi-focused. For instance, many of those who were strongly for remaining in the EU would have liked Britain to take part in a European army which would have freedom of manoeuvre independently of others, most obviously of the U.S.

  However, this is not practical politics for the foreseeable future.

- Britain should stay well armed but not a member of any alliances or entanglements with the outside world. It should be prepared to defend itself at any time, and indeed be in perpetual readiness, but not otherwise involve itself in any possibility of conflict.

  This is Swedish-Swiss style neutralism, which some do advocate for Britain.[1]

---

[1] Though Sweden has started moving away from this tradition in recent years

- Britain should free itself from all military alliances and largely disarm. It should henceforth pursue a peaceful role in the world, mostly through the UN.

  This of course is the viewpoint associated with the left. We are going to advocate something different to all of these, though with elements in common with several:

- Britain should reorientate its foreign policy to place less emphasis on military alliances and confrontation with selected opponents, and more emphasis on conflict resolution and international security and peacekeeping. We hope for a future in which Britain is recognised as a leading member of the larger world community both for its constructive initiatives and its contribution to agreed international peacekeeping forces.

Our option is not an immediate world peace option, obviously. It is not even a long-term aim to call for abandonment of all armed forces. After all, if one day there is a world authority in charge of international peace and security, it would have to have a muscular arm to enforce international decisions against the truculent, and this is exactly the sort of thing which Britain should contribute to. We call only for a very cautious start, which would at least be in sympathy with an aim of eventual world order rather than downright antagonistic to it. After all, this is what was once claimed by many people, and not just idealistic leftists,

---

to be the long-term aim once the cold war could be brought to an end.

The 1918 legacy

The twentieth century was dominated by the First World War and its later consequences. It installed lunatic-fringe extremists into power in Russia, and other lunatic-fringe extremists (after a few years) in Germany. The German result led to a second war only 21 years after the first. The Russian outcome lasted until the ending of Soviet communism in 1991. Not that this ending turned out to be a release of the world into sunlit uplands when it finally happened. Rather the world's leaders, with an almost audible sigh of relief, returned to business as usual pre-1914 style, and with enthusiasm.

Yet there had been something new after the ending of WW1. It contained some posturing but there was something genuine as well. The victors set up the League of Nations and invited the rest of the world to join. It foundered on fascism and communism, but the United Nations after the Second World War took over its essential features and its underlying ideals. People had expressed ideas of an international security order and world peace before, but it had never been proclaimed in all seriousness quite like this.

The world soon had other things on its plate than this long-term ideal, yet it was never put away even by the most routine politicians. Even as war after war was fought in the years since 1918, it was proclaimed again and again, in Britain and America and all their allies, that rule-based world order was the long-term aim. If only, and when, all those evils abroad, particularly expansionist communism, and after 1945, some of the newer nationalisms and ideologies, when at last these were finally banished, then however much it had been postponed, one day the long-term ideals would re-emerge triumphant.It was genuine once, but by the time it became possible it was a lie.

Meanwhile in Britain...

In Britain present-day foreign policy really dates from Suez in 1956, though it's more often said that it dates from 1945. That was when the Second World War ended (and simultaneously the nuclear age started), and Britain came out of it, victorious, but so weakened that that it had lost its status as a major power. As one author remarked, it didn't take much perceptiveness to notice that a war which had started as a quarrel between Europeans was ended by the Americans and Russians.

American troops meet Russian counterparts in Berlin (Source: The National WWII Museum, New Orleans [1])

But for most of the British establishment (by which we mean the main wings of the two governing parties, the civil service, most people of influence in law and industry, and most newspapers) it took the eleven years till Suez before they cottoned on, at least about the loss of great power status. Following the nationalisation of the Suez canal by the (vehemently anti-western) Egyptian president Nasser, Britain and France dispatched military forces to seize the canal (and oust Nasser), though they insisted it wasn't a war but a 'police operation'.[2] But they hadn't consulted the Americans, who were furious and joined the Soviets and others in condemnation, and put economic sanctions on Britain which immediately forced a climbdown by the prime minister Sir Anthony Eden.

For things like colonial independence, it was different, for that had begun before WW2 with things like the Statute of Westminster in 1931 which recognised dominion status as independence, and a clear commitment to moving the colonies in that direction. It was also recognised that the USA and the Soviet Union were now the most major powers. But none of this was accompanied by doubts that Britain itself was still a major power in the same league. It was simply instinctive, for instance, for the Atlee government to go ahead with a British nuclear bomb,

---

[1] https://www.nationalww2museum.org/war/articles/what-will-russia-do-after-war

[2] Does that remind you of anything at the present time?

insisting, in the famous words of Nye Bevan, that it 'had to have a bloody-great Union Jack stamped on it.' It was equally instinctive for Sir Anthony Eden to consider it a British responsibility to act against usurpers of the international order like Nasser, just as it had been the British responsibility to act against Hitler. Nobody blamed the lesser countries of the world for not taking action, for that was the prerogative and duty of great powers like Britain (albeit in alliance with others). And of course, the due order which Nasser was usurping was itself the creation of Britain and the other powers of significance.

It's worth emphasising the sheer shock power which Suez had on British thinking. Everybody watched as a British government, and a Conservative government at that, was told by America to stop this nonsense and behave themselves (in pretty-well those words), and meekly obeyed. And the Suez effect went beyond politics. Within a year every aspect of British culture, life and style seemed to have been affected, as if by a life-changing trauma. 1956 was the year not only of Suez but also of the 'Angry Young Men', with plays like John Osborne's 'Look Back in Anger', of new artists and designers, all of whom seemed to emphasis their radical renunciation of the British past.

In retrospect these new forces must have been there for years, but the Suez debacle was the catalyst. And it went on for years, in fact is still going on in many ways. One of the favourite sayings of the day was a remark by the American Secretary of State Dean Ascherson that 'Great Britain has lost an empire but not yet found a role.' This remark was endlessly recycled in the media with non-stop articles and programmes about Britain's shock loss of power and what its future now held. For years after 1956 the media seemed unable to stop going on and on forever about it.

In the end things settled down to a consensus (among the establishment at least) about, not a single role, but a multi-faceted role, with several elements. First, and quickly the most sacrosanct, was agreement that the American alliance, albeit an alliance in which Britain was the subordinate member, was crucial for British security (never mind security against whom, just security). You might have thought that resentment against America would be a major feature in Britain after what happened at Suez, and there was a little for a while, but it soon died away. Towards the end of the 1950s Harold Macmillan made a remark about Britain being the Greeks to America's Romans, and that caught the general spirit of the attitude which continues to this day. Other facets to the role were to be complementary to the American subordination and would have to be secondary to it and give way to it if there was any inconsistency.

Ensuring there was no such inconsistency, there was the wider western alliance, meaning Nato (North Atlantic Treaty Organisation). Nato was formed in a panic in 1948, when after Stalin's installation of communist governments in 'his' part of Europe there was real fear that it would be easy for him to move into the rest of Europe and impose the same. In the circumstances this fear was not totally irrational, but the consequence was the division of the world into two confronting blocs with weapons of mass destruction poised for instant use. This, the Cold War, has been the most prominent feature of the world since 1945.

The third element was the British independent nuclear deterrent. In a way this is an anomaly, for it is a unilateral element contrary to the pattern of alliances and mutual dependencies which is the rest of the British defence posture. Its supporters claim that it's a last-resort scenario, the ultimate just-in-case, to be maintained forever just because you never can be sure exactly what might or might not happen one day. Rewording that, it is intended to be maintained forever *irrespective* of what might or might not ever happen. Clearly, countries which take that attitude (and Britain is not the only one) are blocking any attempt towards world nuclear arms control.

US President Harry Truman signing the original Nato agreement on 4th April 1949 (Source: BBC[1])

[1] BBC (2022), Nato: What is the North Atlantic Treaty Organisation? 18th February, https://www.bbc.co.uk/newsround/60416721

An apparently more moderate version of support for the British independent deterrent is to claim, not that it must be there forever irrespective of all other considerations, but that it's required until there can be world agreement on a nuclear disarmament regime. This is the famous 'multilateralist' argument saying, 'Yes, we believe in nuclear disarmament too, but there's no point abandoning our nuclear weapons if nobody else does the same, so we are waiting till international disarmament negotiations can start.' For very many years this was the favoured response of most politicians to calls for nuclear disarmament, not only the main wing of Labour MPs for whom the major motive was to ward off criticism from the left, but of Conservatives as well. We can still remember when a leading Conservative of the day began his answer to a question on the BBC's Question Time with the words "Us multilateralists..."

If it was sincere, it would be a decent argument. But history since the collapse of Soviet communism shows beyond doubt that it is, and must always have been, grossly insincere. Both main political parties have had their years in power since 1992, and both did not merely not take any action towards the launch of any such negotiations, but deliberately and cynically obstructed every attempt by others to do so. For years a number of countries in the UN General Assembly made repeated attempts to remind the nuclear powers of the obligations they entered into under Clause 6 of the Non-Proliferation Treaty of 1968, in which the nuclear powers pledged to engage in international nuclear disarmament talks in exchange of all other countries refraining from acquiring nuclear weapons. But it was always thrown out by the nuclear powers using their domination of the Security Council, giving any reason or none, e.g., 'this is not the correct forum,' and 'the time is not yet ripe'. The in-your-face perfunctoriness of the excuses says it all about the attitude.

It's a pity it was just a con, for multilateral nuclear disarmament is crucial for the future for a rules-based international order.

The independent deterrent has its critics inside Britain; it is the most vulnerable part of the British security posture. Even among conservatives one sometimes detects some discreet doubt about it. Admittedly there are doubts expressed by other conservatives which are from the opposite point of view. These doubts are that it's not sufficiently independent but rather, too heavily reliant on the Americans. The present and future-planned deterrent involves a small fleet of submarines armed with delivery missiles with nuclear bombs on them, and the submarines are British built, and the warheads are British built, but the delivery system is American. A lot of debate is about whether the missiles could actually be launched without the permission of the Americans, though in view of the apocalyptic circumstances necessary for them to launched that seems a relatively minor consideration. More to the point is that if one day the Americans decided that they didn't want Britain to have an independent deterrent any more they could enforce their will by stopping the supply and maintenance of the missiles.

The independent deterrent is not greatly loved but is maintained as a kind of lowest common denominator of what the practising politicians can agree on. It is also seriously expensive to maintain, in a country that tends to regard itself as in almost permanent economic and financial crisis. Our own guess is that it will come to an end one day when the Americans, for whatever reason, decide to pull the plug on it. Britain though is probably the only country that the Americans could force such a thing upon. It is unlikely they could force the French in the same way, and obviously couldn't force the Russians or Chinese, or any of the newer nuclear powers, as nuclear weapons spread inevitably around the world. Any move towards multilateral nuclear disarmament is going to need more than transient support from one American administration, even if there was any sign of any so-minded administration appearing but will have to be consequent on successful moves to resolve the present tensions between major powers.

The fourth element of new thinking after Suez was Europe. The European Common Market had already been launched, but Britain stood aloof. Now Britain was interested. And though it was still technically only a common market, the federalist aspiration was already there. Indeed, this was the attraction for many who were now vehement that Britain's future was in Europe: the outmoded nationalisms of Europe, British included, were to be subsumed by a new European identity.

By now it's clear that this element of the vision hasn't worked. Before the European referendum, when Britain was still in Europe and few thought it would leave, nevertheless you'd have been hard put to find anyone who said they regarded their national identity as primarily European as opposed to British, English, Scots or Northern

Irish/Irish/Ulster. It was the same on the continent where people continued to regard themselves as primarily French, German or whatever, and still do. With this element having failed, and though we were still surprised by the referendum result, we were less surprised than we might have been – the opponents of Europe could appeal to feelings of national identity, but the supporters couldn't appeal to feelings of a different national identity, so had to fall back on indecisive economic arguments. For the time being and for better or worse, renewed Europeanism is not practical politics.

After communism: new enemies for old

In the mid 1980s the thing happened which the world had been waiting for: communist reformers came to power in the Soviet Union. This time there could be no intervention by a dominant communist power from outside to force things back to orthodoxy, as had happened in Hungary in 1956 and Czechoslovakia in 1968. This at long last could be the unravelling of the damage to the world caused by the First World War. You'd have thought there'd be nothing but joy in the west as the reality sank in.

Anything but. The initial response by key western governments was open refusal to recognise that anything much had genuinely happened, that anything had changed at all. It seemed that the leaders (most obviously Margaret Thatcher in Britain and Ronald Regan in the US) were too comfortable with their certainties in the cold war and didn't want any change. They didn't put it quite that baldly, but whenever the matter was put to them about the change in the Soviet Union all their emphasis was negative: the changes were only modest, what they were could easily be reversed, and so on. In the end, after a long time, Margaret Thatcher was persuaded to say that Gorbachev was a man 'she could do business with.' Her admirers have claimed since that this showed early prescience of how things had changed, but the opposite was the case. The remark was wrung out of her very reluctantly and very tardily.

Even at the time this looked like a bad sign; in retrospect it was a very bad sign indeed. During the Cold War (meaning the period when the major confrontation in the world was between the west and the Soviet Union), most of us managed to hope that once the ideological difference between the sides was ended, or somehow resolved, there would be real moves towards creating an international security order, which was supposed to be the aim of international statecraft since the setting up of the League of Nations after WW1.

But there were cynics, and we had to hope that these cynics were wrong. The cynics said that if you removed one enemy from countries with a great power view of themselves, they would simply find new enemies in place of old; it was like two large animals being put in a cage together, who would soon enough be snarling and then fighting one another.

The alleged longing for world peace (if only the cold war could be ended) was a con, like the multilateral nuclear disarmament con, just a device to quieten feeble minded idealists while the people in charge got on with following their real instincts.

A Cliched View of The Cold War (Source: Australian Institute of International Affairs[1])

The cynics were the ones who were right. When it came to the point where there was at last a chance of reaching for the ideals they'd claimed for 70 years – sincere moves towards a real international order, real and serious international disarmament negotiations – when the chance came at last, and when there were no more reasons for postponement, they didn't want to know. This is the great betrayal of our time.

---

[1] Switzer, T. (2018), Russiaphobia and the Perils of a New Cold War, Australian Institute of International Affairs, 18th April https://www.internationalaffairs.org.au/australianoutlook/russiaphobia-perils-new-cold-war/

Chapter 2

Not the Peace Dividend

The peace dividend

By 1990 almost all politicians in the west were prepared to accept that something had changed in the Soviet Union. Some extreme hawks weren't having it – Dick Cheney who 10 years later was to be George W. Bush's Vice-President, still maintained, apparently, that Gorbachev was just another communist; and there were some others like him. But the mainstream was suddenly proclaiming that the Cold War was over.

So, was an era of world peace about to break out? For sure the word 'caution' was still almost every second word of the politicians in power in the west, and it was clear there was very little intention of any really drastic disarmament in the foreseeable future. But on the positive side the phrase 'the peace dividend' had made its appearance by the end of the 1980s, and the people who used it seem to have been genuine about it as far as it went. It meant that there could at least be a reduction in arms spending, and that the money saved could be spent on things like social programmes and economic development.

As it happened this was a disappointment even in its own terms. Clearly it would entail the 'swords into ploughshares' sort of planning that people had spoken of for as long as disarmament negotiations between nations had existed, but little took place. By 1993 there were complaints that no effort had been made to plan any such thing.[1] The complaint was that when a government plan for redeployment of defence work into other areas was needed, almost nothing was forthcoming, which left companies dependent on defence work to their own devices about restructuring and diversifying. Some were trying to diversify, but some were simply contracting, and abandoning areas of work, and with it abandoning the workers who were dependent on that work.

Partly this was simply the spirit of the times (of which more in the next chapter). The immediate aftermath of the collapse of Soviet communism spilled over into attitudes towards everything associated with it, and the early 1990s was the time when the devotees of free-market economics were heady with triumph. This was the period when any time you looked at a newspaper you saw pictures of free-market economists, journalists and members of right-wing think-tanks (often looking distinctly weird in bow ties and the like), setting off for speaking tours of the ex-communist countries to the east, where they were often getting rapturous responses into the bargain. Even the Soviet Union (which existed until 1991) was swept along with it. Any voices of caution were dismissed. When the Soviet Union proceeded to plunge under the effect of the reckless rush from one economic extreme to the other, and people asked if the west could not give aid to Russia, the typical western

---

[1] See for instance 'What happened to the peace dividend...?' by Andrew Marshall, The Independent, 3rd January 1993

response was that a little bit of such aid could be considered, provided it was used 'to kick-start a free market'. This revealing and brutal phrase was used repeatedly at the time, with no sign of irony or even black humour.

So, it was no surprise that the adjustment of large sections of the British economy to a reduction in arms spending was left to the free-market rather than government action. As it happened it hardly mattered, for the reduction in arms spending hardly came through. An academic paper published in 1996 made the point that when the defence budgets of the early 90s were measured against the average over the cold war, there were hardly any cuts at all. 'Thus, given the current secure West European military environment and the disarmament measures introduced in the East, it is difficult not to conclude that the UK reductions in defence spending since 1984-85 remain modest.'[1]

Of course, all this is forgotten by the time we're writing. The alleged peace dividend was a tardy response to events that were already history, and political attitudes even at the time were to ensure it would be swept away.

To Reykjavik and back

When Mikhail Gorbachev became secretary-general of the Soviet Communist Party in 1985 (and hence de facto leader of the Soviet Union) he began making disarmament overtures to the west almost immediately, even before it

[1] Ian Davis, 'the UK Peace Dividend...', University of Bradford 1996

became clear that he was also an internal reformer. At first it looked as if this was falling on hopelessly barren ground.

Mikhail Gorbachev with Ronald Reagan in Background Source: History.info[1]

His opposite number in the U.S. was Ronald Reagan, a fierce conservative who had assumed office in 1981, and had campaigned on a ticket of ratcheting up confrontation with the Soviet Union, which he famously referred to as the 'evil empire'.

[1] 1985: Gorbachev Becomes General Secretary of the Communist Party and Leader of the Soviet Union, https://history.info/on-this-day/1985-gorbachev-general-secretary-communist-party-leader-soviet-union/

Unsurprisingly the only response at first to Gorbachev was to insist that armed face-off would continue so long as the Soviet Union did not change its character. He wasn't to know that this was exactly what Gorbachev had in mind.

So, Reagan remained obdurate at first, continuing with the massive arms build up characteristic of his initial years. But rather to the surprise of many people he then agreed to meet Gorbachev for a summit in Geneva in 1985, and there seems to have been personally taken by him, reportedly finding him a great contrast to previous Soviet politicians he had met, who had been unendingly stony-faced, buttoned-up and hostile.

But more, both sides had something new to say. Gorbachev was an unknown quantity at the time, but you might have expected the right-wing Reagan to be a staunch advocate of the doctrine of massive nuclear deterrence, frequently known, at least at that time, as MAD (Mutually Assured Deterrence). It meant that if either side attacked the other there would be instant and devastating nuclear retaliation which would totally destroy the aggressor.

It would destroy the rest of the world as well of course, but the theory was that the deterrent effect of knowing this would so deter any attack that world peace would be kept. How long for, whether there would never be any attack on a major power again for the rest of human history, things like that were left vague, but most right-wingers in the west were vehement that this was the way to maintain world peace.

You would certainly have expected Reagan to be a believer in massive nuclear deterrence. But there was a surprise in store, at least for those who didn't know Reagan's personal history on such matters. He declared himself a sceptic of MAD, certainly as a method of ensuring world peace for evermore and believed himself to have a radically different alternative. Unfortunately, it was an alternative which in turn was totally unacceptable to the Soviets, even under Gorbachev.

Reagan committed himself to a programme called 'Strategic Defense[1] Initiative', an intensification of so-called missile defence – that is, anti-missile missiles which would shoot down hostile missiles on their way to their targets.

The anti-missile missile was already an old idea, and the U.S. and Soviet Union had negotiated the ABM (Anti-Ballistic Missile) treaty as early as 1972, whose purpose was actually to ban such developments because they were seen as destabilising to the balance of terror that was the nuclear stalemate.

Any country which could shoot down its opponents' missiles would obviously be in a position to use their own missiles to overpower their opponents.

---

[1] American spelling will be used when appropriate

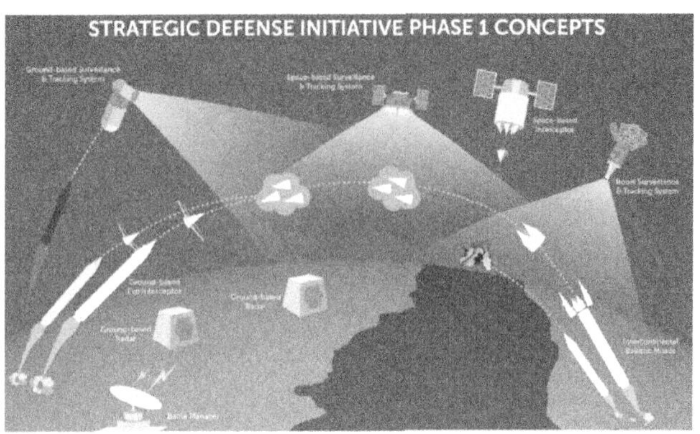

US "Star Wars" Strategic Defense Initiative proposed by President Reagan in 1983 (Source: MissileThreat[1])

Partly the opposition of most of the defence establishment to the very idea of anti-missile missiles was the extreme unlikelihood if their effectiveness ever being 100%, in a situation in which it would have to be 100% against nuclear-carrying missiles. But a minority of right-wingers, carried away by instinctive belief in American technical genius and the general technophilia which marks the American right, had continued to lobby for it. Reagan himself had been convinced years before of such technical fixes, having spoken in the 1960s to Edward Teller, the

[1] Williams, I., Karako, T. and Rumbaugh, W. (2017), Missile Defense 2020: Next Steps for Defending the Homeland, MissileThreat , CSIS Missile Defense Project April 7th https://missilethreat.csis.org/missile-defense-2020/

physicist sometimes called the 'Father of the H-bomb' – and was said to be the original inspiration for Dr Strangelove, famously played by Peter Sellers in the film of that name. Teller behaved just as you'd expect of Dr Strangelove, showing a fantastical love of nuclear weapons and always calling for more and more of them, and more and more nuclear testing. He even advocated the routine use of H-bombs for civilian purposes, giving as an example the excavation of a harbour.

But Reagan's Strategic Defense Initiative, as inspired by Teller, was a twist on the mere anti-missile missile, because the idea was a system that would shoot down enemy missiles in space. It became popularly known as 'Star Wars' after the SF film of that name. As such it was an early precursor to the militarisation of space that was to become most associated with the Bush administration of 2001-9. Reagan declared himself to be so total an advocate of SDI that he refused to envisage any agreement with the Soviets which did not include it. As a mark of his belief that it was the true alternative to MAD, and his sincerity that it was a purely defensive system, he even offered to share SDI knowhow and technology with the Soviets. But the Soviets were having none of proposals that from their point of view would grossly upset the balance between the two sides. In the end Reagan and Gorbachev could only agree to try again at Reykjavik a year later.

The Reykjavik summit of 1986 also failed, and for the same reason. Again, it foundered on Reagan's determination that he was going to press ahead with 'Star Wars' and the Soviet determination that they would permit nothing of such an attempt to upset the balance of weaponry between the two sides. Yet this summit has a strange, perverse reputation in the history of international relations, for it is regarded as the occasion when hostility between he US and the Soviet Union finally evaporated. For it was when both sides acknowledged that both leaders seriously spoke of world-wide abolition of nuclear weapons. This was astonishing for a right-wing conservative.

In Britain the prime minister Margaret Thatcher was horrified. Here was someone who was certainly a believer in nuclear weapons as the ultimate deterrent. Not for her the peculiar abhorrence of nuclear weapons which is usual among liberals and left-wingers. For her nuclear weapons were the ultimate security – the conservative MP Lady Olga Maitland who claimed the reason she was able to sleep at night was because of Britain's nuclear weapons spoke perfectly on behalf of Margaret Thatcher too. By all reports when Margaret Thatcher heard of the sentiments Ronald Reagan had expressed at Reykjavik about ridding the world of nuclear weapons, she first expressed incredulity, then betrayal. How could someone who'd been so close to her politically, even calling each other by first names, regarded internationally as almost an item – how could he do this to her?

Thatcher and Reagan at Camp David in 1986 (Source: *Guardian*[1])

And the ally she thought she was so close to had acted without any consultation with her, or even informing her what was going on. Eventually a phone call from her was set up to Ronald Reagan, a senior member of her staff listened and took notes, and both the archive of Thatcher papers which was released in recent years and an American account which was released almost immediately, agree on the strange things Reagan said.[2]

In the phone call Margaret Thatcher put her emphasis not on her attitude to nuclear weapons in general but

---

[1] Wheatcroft, G. (2014), 'The Thatcher-Reagan love affair wasn't all plain sailing', *Guardian*, 10th November, https://www.theguardian.com/commentisfree/2014/nov/10/margaret-thatcher-ronald-reagan-love-affair-churchill-roosevelt

[2] See any relevant press cutting from the time; also, the archive of Margaret Thatcher papers released at the end of 2015 (https://www.margaretthatcher.org/archive/1986tna1)

concern about the alleged imbalance of conventional forces in Europe which was thought to greatly favour the Soviets, and which western nuclear forces were supposed to counterbalance. Reagan replied that that could be dealt with because the Soviets 'don't want war; they want victory by the threat of nuclear war.' When Margaret Thatcher persisted in her protests, he then told her to read a thriller by Tom Clancy which, he said, gave an excellent picture of Soviet intentions and strategy. What Margaret Thatcher thought of that suggestion seems not to have been recorded.

In fact, Gorbachev's intentions seem to have been what they claimed to be; everything which has emerged since then seems to confirm it. It is Reagan's intentions which are the puzzle. This archconservative had suddenly taken a CND-type attitude to nuclear weapons but simultaneously sabotaged it by digging his heels in about SDI which he knew the Soviets would not accept. He had warmed to Gorbachev personally at the two summits, yet the thriller he commended to Margaret Thatcher depicted the Soviet leader as a fraud who was only pretending to be a reformer in order to fool the west about his real diabolical intentions. Was Reagan sending a subtle message to Margaret Thatcher that he didn't genuinely trust Gorbachev but was engaging in some ruse of his own? If so what ruse? What would he gain, since his political appeal was to the militant right? But since when were either Reagan or Thatcher subtle? Even senior members of Reagan's own team told reporters they were baffled about what their boss was up to. Whatever his intentions the effect was that the two summits came to nothing, and Margaret Thatcher and others were saved from the horrors of peace.

But the increase – for a while – in trust between the Soviet Union and USA is generally considered a positive from the meeting. More traditionally minded negotiations for arms control continued, and 5 years after Reykjavik the first START (Strategic Arms Reduction Treaty) was signed, in which both sides agreed to limit the number of nuclear warheads on their missiles to a mere 6,000 each. (No that's not a joke: they agreed to a limit of merely 6,000 nuclear warheads each.) The world continued on what was perhaps its pre-ordained path, a fact which may be a theoretical gratification to Marxists and others who believe that history is pre-determined by inexorable factors but is regrettable to the rest of us.

The champs

In 1991 old-style communists in the Soviet Union made a last despairing effort to resurrect orthodox communist rule, by attempting to overthrow Gorbachev in a palace revolution similar to the one which overthrew Khrushchev in 1964. It failed miserably, and interestingly too, for it showed how beneath the conformist surface reformist ideas were now widespread in the Soviet Union, even inside the Communist party itself. This too was reminiscent of post-war history, namely Hungary in 1956 and Czechoslovakia in 1968. But there was one sense in which the orthodox communists turned out to be right, though one can argue about whether it was a self-fulfilling prophesy: communism itself did not survive the attempt to reconcile it with democracy.

The break was epitomised by Boris Yeltsin, originally a party apparatchik but who had put himself so out front in his reformist enthusiasm that he was disciplined by the Moscow party. When the attempted coup came, he seized the opportunity, being photographed by the world on top of a tank proclaiming his defiance. When the coup failed this was Yeltsin's opportunity, and he took it.

Moscow coup 1991 When Yeltsin Addressed the Russian People Source: Reuters[1])

Almost immediately, and despite the fact that the coup had been an attempt to oust him and had failed, Gorbachev was regarded as somehow disgraced by it, and forced to resign as leader of the Communist Party. Yeltsin became president of Russia, though for a short time Gorbachev remained president of the larger Soviet Union. But then, in a move which was extraordinary even by what became his

[1] Sandford, D. (2011), 'Moscow coup 1991: With Boris Yeltsin on the tank', BBC News, 20th August, https://www.bbc.co.uk/news/world-europe-14589691

own standards, Yeltsin got rid of Gorbachev by dissolving the Soviet Union itself. Already the Baltic states, which had been annexed by Stalin as part of his 1939 deal with Hitler, had been pushing to leave, and the Asian and Caucasian states were happy enough to agree as well, if only as a means, in some of them, to continue the old communist leadership in a new guise.

What followed was not the best side of human nature and can be seen as the genesis of events leading up to the recent situation in Ukraine in 2022.

With few exceptions the newly released countries of the ex-Soviet Union and eastern Europe promptly went on an anti-Russian kick reminiscent of the anti-colonialist anti-imperialist kick which had dominated the UN and the Commonwealth for a generation after 1960. As they saw it, Russia had taken control of them and imposed regimes on them that were the very exemplar of 20th century totalitarianism – not only dictatorship, not only censorship of the press, but the banning of all press except government publications, not just rule by the Communist party, but an omnipresence of the Communist party in every aspect of every person's life, so that every workplace, every block of flats had its party official whose job was to keep an eye on the occupants.

All that was true, and no exaggeration either. It was also true that it was other Russians who came along and released them, but gratitude for that never became a noticeable feature of their behaviour. Within a year of release it was remarkable how very right-wing they now were. This was shown by their receptiveness to free-market extremism, but more, they chose to assert their new freedom by joining Nato, and not merely joining Nato but doing what they could to make Nato explicitly and vitriolically anti-Russian.

Meanwhile Russia under Yeltsin went into total decline. Yeltsin may have been an early reformer and the hero who led defeat of the attempted coup, but in office he was a drunkard and a danger. Incidents involving him became at best a public joke, as when he lurched onto a stage at some event and joined in playing the bongo drums, and a gross embarrassment like when he was supposed to stop over in Ireland on a plane journey, and the Irish government lined up on the tarmac to meet him, but he was too drunk to get off the plane. But some of his capricious behaviour was more serious. When the Russian parliament rejected some measures of his, he tried to arrest the leaders of the refusers, Charles 1st style. The parliament reacted by arming itself and acted as besieged, whereupon Yeltsin had the parliament building shelled. His troops then moved in and arrested the ringleaders of his opponents. That Russia escaped civil war was pure luck.

Russia became a semi-gangster state as Yeltsin swung into mass privatisation of everything in sight, resulting in a few individuals (including his own family) who had the contacts, initiative and ruthlessness to seize the chance, taking over almost the entire economy, particularly the energy sector, and becoming multi-billionaires. The oligarchs, as these characters became known, came to symbolise the new Russia at home, and also abroad since they bought up various western assets as well, and moved *en masse* into the western property market. Demands for action against 'dirty money' and general buy-ups by foreign criminals have been prominent in the west ever since.

It was into this atmosphere that the phrase, 'The west won the cold war,' became a standard cliché in the western media. It originated with the militaristic right whose central thinking remained attachment to nuclear deterrence, and who had first tried to deny that anything of significance had changed in the Soviet Union. When that became undeniable, they switched to claiming that it was nothing to do with communist reformers internally but Reagan's policy of building up arms which, they claimed, had overwhelmed the Soviet Union and brought about the end of communism.

You might defend the phrase, 'The west won the cold war,' as a statement about ideology only, since nearly all ex-communist countries went for western multi-party systems, and even those who did so only in a sham way (for instance Belarus), paid lip service to western ideas of democracy, which says almost as much. But here was a use of language which was calculated to suggest that the west had actually won a military victory over the Soviet Union, and though people knew it was untrue it was a gross encouragement to governing circles in the west to behave as if it was true. The early talk of treating Russia as an equal soon gave way to an attitude of western hegemony, as the west acted on the assumption of cold war victory. And perhaps that made it inevitable in turn that Russia's attitude towards the west became resentment and then animosity.

The turning point seems to have been the First Gulf War, in 1991. When Saddam Hussain invaded Kuwait he aroused a response that went beyond considerations of oil alone (however some opinion perceived it), and the international response was western led.

They did work at first through the UN, and they did invite the support of the Soviet Union (as it still was), but as the counter-invasion of Kuwait developed it became unmistakable that it was barely disguised unilateral action by the US and its allies, with the Soviet Union left as an onlooker.

The west was signalling unmistakably that they were back in default mode: that it was for them to decide what was allowed and what not allowed in this world, and when it was not it was for them to decide on action and carry it out. There'd already been friction in the former Yugoslavia between American and Soviet forces, both ostensibly there in peace-keeping roles; now the gauntlet was thrown down, as the Soviets (and then the Russians) were bound to see it – and the west knew that that was how they were bound to see it – that the west now intended to rule the world.

A destroyed Iraqi tank rests with oil-well fires burning in background during First Gulf War in early March 1991 (Source: David Longstreath / AP published in The Atlantic[1]

Nato expansion

You might suppose that if you lived through historical events that means you would know what happened, or at least have a better idea of what happened than if you had to gather it from historical records and the differing opinions of historians. If so, try figuring out what happened in the mid 1990s when it was announced that Nato was going to continue as a military alliance, and not merely continue but expand to take in the ex-Soviet republics (except Russia itself) and the former satellite states of eastern Europe.

Nobody seems to know how and by whom, where and when, this decision was made to behave like the victors of a military war. For sure Russia itself was not occupied like Germany and Japan in 1945, but short of that the west was now telling the world that it was a victor, as much a victor as if it had been the military victor of a war. There was no significant public discussion of the decision; all the ordinary person in this country saw was a few days of rumours in the media that such a decision was imminent, a number of

---

[1] Taylor, A. (2016), 'Operation Desert Storm: 25 Years Since the First Gulf War', *The Atlantic*, 14th January, https://www.theatlantic.com/photo/2016/01/operation-desert-storm-25-years-since-the-first-gulf-war/424191/

newspaper articles advocating it suddenly appearing, and immediately afterwards the first joinings were announced.

There were certainly mentions though that the decision had been made in the face of concerns expressed by many senior military, political and diplomatic figures in the west (not exactly traditional pacifists or leftists). One particularly worth mentioning was George Kennan, the Truman advisor who is regarded as the architect of the post-Second World War policy of containment of the Soviet Union and its communist allies. He for one expressed strong opposition to a policy which seemed deliberately out to prevent the ending, but rather a device to renew, the standoff between Russia and the west.

The effect on how Russia was bound to react was repeatedly put forward, and there is no possibility at all that the western leaders did not understand this.

As an example of the mini-rash of articles in the press which appeared a little before public announcement of the decision, the following is from the Independent newspaper in early 1994. Commenting on recent free elections in Russia, it says [1]

> *The 12 December vote in Russia has intensified the debate over the inclusion in Nato of the Eastern and Central European democracies. It has been argued that the West should keep clear of such plans because they could provoke a bitter reaction in Russia, which*

---

[1] Timothy Garton Ash, Michael Mertes and Dominique Moïsi, 'Marriageable partners in search of security,' Independent, 3 January 1994.

in turn would weaken its democratic, pro-Western camp.

Yet the uncertainties over Russia's future make the nervousness of its neighbours entirely understandable. In fact it is Russian democrats themselves who warn against these uncertainties.

Could the inclusion of Eastern and Central European democracies be misunderstood as an exclusion or even isolation of Russia? No, provided that such an inclusion is combined with a convincing effort towards a special security partnership with Russia. And it is Russian democrats themselves who say this most clearly. On 10 December, the 45th anniversary of the UN's Universal Declaration of Human Rights, the Russian Foreign Minister, Andrei Kozyrev, said his country aspired to partnership with Nato, not Nato membership.

He also said that it was the sovereign decision of the Eastern and Central Europeans as to which community or alliance they should join. So Western leaders should finally drop the bad old habit of nervously wondering how the "hawks" in Moscow might react, and try to show a little more of the clarity and courage of those who represent democratic Russia.

Legitimate Russian interests do not extend to a right of veto over the security arrangements of the Soviet Union's former satellites – nor indeed of the Baltic states or Ukraine.

A democratic Russia will distinguish itself from the Communist Soviet Union precisely by recognising this truth. In addition, the inclusion of Eastern and Central Europe into Nato is in Russia's own enlightened self-interest. A reinforced Alliance for stability and democracy in Europe will also help the democratic and peaceful forces in Russia. Russia needs stability on its western border, just as we do on our eastern borders.

Notice how the claim that Nato expansion would somehow help the democratic parties in Russia against the autocratic ones is vague, but the enthusiasm for renewed confrontation with Russia is unmistakeable.

Also notice the early appearance of the claim that no country has a right to object to any alliances joined in by its neighbours, and that this is somehow a reason in itself for Russia's neighbours to join Nato.

So where did the decision come from? We know that the newly liberated countries of eastern Europe and the Soviet Union pushed for it as alleged protection from (the equally newly liberated) Russia, but why did the western leaders go along with it?

It has been suggested that the Clinton administration in the US was in favour because they saw Nato as an instrument of American world leadership, and hence of unchallengeable world domination. However, it appears that the Clinton administration was split, with two key members in favour and two against,[1] and it was several years

---

[1] Jane M O Sharp, "British views on Nato enlargement," a Nato-funded paper 1997https://www.nato.int/acad/conf/enlarg97/sharp.htm

before the US officially came down in favour. Britain obediently followed, and so did other western governments.

Source: Center for Strategic and International Studies (CSIS)[1]

It is reasonable to assume that the Nato secretariat in Brussels was in favour, since it is usually instinctive for the people who run large organisations to want to expand them, with equal expansion of their own roles and well-paid jobs; however, we have not found material about what went on behind the scenes at that time. (Today in 2022 the Nato secretariat is utterly hard line about Nato's God-given right to expand and opposed to any compromise about it.) Of course, technically Nato is run by its member governments, but the practice is not like that. Like the UN, it behaves as an entity in its own right; it has its own diplomatic representatives to countries and organisations, its own flag,

---

[1] CSIS (2017), NATO Enlargement — A Case Study, Center for Strategic and International Studies, May 15th , https://medium.com/center-for-strategic-and-international-studies/nato-enlargement-a-case-study-c380545dd38d

and certainly its own interests – and for years now it has made it clear that its paramount interest is expansion. It even has its own phrase for it: 'Nato to find a role.'

When intervention took place in Bosnia and later in Kosovo Nato pushed to 'find a role', and was soon granted its wish, and when these interventions seemed to falter, another phrase that was heard and seen everywhere was that 'the important thing is that Nato must not be seen to fail.' Since then, Nato has also 'found a role' in Afghanistan and Iraq, Somalia and Libya, (and the list is not exhaustive). By now it is accepted that Nato watches every part of the world for nascent conflicts, and whenever it can see something promising it seeks to 'find a role'. This role is usually expressed as 'peace-keeping operations', but that is Orwellian language, for they seek to be deployed in an active military capacity. Peace means war.

So, after one escape from the world annihilating itself through its own conflicts plus too much scientific skill, a new quarrel was deliberately started, originally about (literally) nothing whatsoever, and has taken off.

But are we really saying that it's just a few wicked people, say in Nato headquarters, who are out to start wars so as to boost their own positions and salaries, a few half-crazed militarists on the far right, a number of journalists who for years now are appearing in the media unmistakably gagging for war? Or on the other side, that it's wicked Russians running a gangster state, motivated by fears that their ill-gotten gains could be threatened, and the claim that Nato is a danger to them really the fear of democracy being brought to Russia's doorstep?

But why does it keep happening? They allegedly overcame the bad guys in 1918 and the world was told there could now be a new internationalist peaceful order. But it got interrupted by having to overcome another lot of bad guys 20 years later, and after 1945 there were another lot of bad guys who, if they couldn't be overcome, had to be confronted. Eventually better guys took over in the Soviet Union, but unfortunately by then there were more bad guys in the middle east and elsewhere. And then there were bad guys in Russia again. What keeps going wrong?

Chapter 3

Climates of Ideas

The title of this chapter is a cliché, but like most clichés it is about a truth. The actions of countries are caused by the way the people of influence think. We know this yet it is sometimes hard to believe, as we witness the hardware of their power and positions, the limousines, the armed guards, the military parades, the gigantic firepower – all based on the software of habits and precedencies, personal relationships, currents of opinion, right down to the gossip in their clubs; this plus the awesome ability of humans to organise and engage in massive industrial production. This is not an academic book but let us take look at some themes in their thinking during the period when the national leaders turned the enormous hope presented to the world in 1989-1991 into its complete reversal of more great power rivalries, confrontations and threats of war.

Spheres of hegemony

Any reading of the discussions at the time of the Nato enlargement decision in the 1990s, at the level of governments, diplomats and generals and other people of influence in the west, brings out how 19th century their ideas were. For instance, in the Nato funded paper by Jane MO Sharp, referred to in the last chapter, you find the following paragraph:

Lord Ismay, NATO's first Secretary General, said in the 1940s that the three main advantages of NATO for western Europe were that "it kept the Americans in, the Russians out and the Germans down." This would not be a politically correct rendering today, but for Britain it remains essential to keep the United States engaged in Europe to balance the potential power and influence of Russia. With respect to Germany, while no one in Tony Blair's government would speak of keeping Germany down, it is considered vital (in Bonn as well as in London) to keep Germany tied to the western democracies and to the institutions of the western security community; both NATO and the EU. If Germany believes it important to bring Poland, the Czech Republic and Hungary into NATO, that is reason enough for Britain. For if NATO were to deny membership to the central Europeans, then eventually either Germany or Russia would fill the role of hegemonic protector, thereby returning Europe back to the uncertainties of the 1930s.

This disturbing glimpse into the mindset of people at the highest levels of western decision-making at the time pretty well says it all. The reason the world returned to business as usual pre-1914 style after the collapse of Soviet communism is that mentally these people were still in the pre-1914 world. Obviously, they had noticed the events of the 20th century in the literal sense of noticing, but they interpreted the events in terms of what was to them the eternal order: the inevitable struggle between rivals for power, influence and hegemony. Never mind ideology like communism and its rivals, and the ideals to which they were supposed to be committed since 1919 (though lip service would be paid when requested). To the sensible people who ran things (themselves), it was always and ever about the inevitable struggle for domination between the countries and blocs who were the strongest. If Russian hegemony over eastern Europe had suddenly ended, for whatever reason, then this was the opportunity to press eastern Europe into their own sphere of hegemony. Indeed, they had to, for if they didn't then it would fall into someone else's sphere of hegemony. This view of history and what humanity should be about was the default outlook of those responsible for Nato enlargement.

The publicly stated reasons that were given for Nato expansion (though no effort was made to hide the background assumptions) were anodyne, unarguable but vacuous. Nato's own publications speak of Nato adding security guarantees to countries which are suitable by virtue of being democracies and so on; here is a list of requirements for all countries 'which share the alliance's values' which is a little more explicit, published by the US State Department and released in 2001:[1]

- *New members must uphold democracy, including tolerating diversity*
- *New members must be making progress toward a market economy*

---

[1] https://1997-2001.state.gov/regions/eur/fs_members.html. Though not a Nato paper, it can be taken as speaking pretty well on behalf of Nato.

- *Their military forces must be under firm civilian control*
- *They must be good neighbors and respect sovereignty outside their borders*
- *They must be working toward compatibility with NATO forces*

Leaving aside the inclusion of progress toward a market economy, as if free markets are a freedom of the same sort as freedom of speech or free elections, which is a tribute to the triumphalist right-wing atmosphere which had now developed, the significant part is the clear hint contained in 'They must be good neighbors and respect sovereignty outside their borders'. Everyone picks up the reference of course: Russia does not do this, so is opposed by Nato, so countries which join Nato must oppose Russia.

The criticism of Russia is that Russia (or at least Putin) is motivated by its own sphere-of-hegemony ambitions, in the form of a desire to recreate the Soviet Union, or at least dominate the area it used to cover. Well, they should know, since this is the mirror image of exactly what Nato set out to do from the 1990s onwards. Nato started it (well before anyone had heard of Putin), and there is no serious doubt that the primary and long-term cause of Russian misbehaviour is Nato expansion initiated in the 1990s.

Vladimir Putin addresses the Russian defence ministry board (Source: Mikhail Tereshchenko/AP[1])

Deterrence

The First World War had a profound effect on the thinking of people afterwards, leading to a massive dread of any repetition of the experience. The 'appeasement' of Hitler by Chamberlain and others is often attributed to this. In the 1930s there was a belief among many people that a second war would be pretty well the end of the world: it was thought that the population would be massacred from the air, vast areas would be poisoned by gas (perhaps for evermore, with the gas spreading remorselessly across the globe), biological agents would destroy what the gas had not, the organised

---

[1] Roth, A. *2021), 'Putin warns of possible military response over 'aggressive' Nato', *Guardian,* 21st December, https://www.theguardian.com/world/2021/dec/21/putin-warns-of-possible-military-response-to-aggressive-nato-russia

civil state would be eliminated, that starving, poisoned and infectious masses would fall under the control of local strongmen in the way that early monarchs had arisen, and so on.

As it happened the Second World War didn't turn out to be quite so cataclysmic (though it's easy to say that writing in a country which escaped the worst of the war devastation). But the fact that the worst predictions didn't happen led to post war attitudes which went too far in the opposite direction. The next generation of politicians came out of the war far too sanguine about the new weapons of mass destruction.

There is a surprising lack of awareness of just how narrow a miss the Second World War was. Nuclear weapons were finally ready just, and only just, as the conflict was ending as a conventional war, weeks after Germany had already surrendered leaving only Japan to be the first (and so far only) country to be nuked. If nuclear weapons had been ready in 1942 for instance, imagine what might have followed. But it didn't happen, the perception was that the Second World War had not been the total disaster pre-war Jeremias had prophesied, and post war politicians readily embraced the new weapons. And when they were challenged, they came up with the argument from deterrence.

The claim that we need nuclear weapons as a deterrent to others, because these others also had nuclear weapons, was a *post facto* justification – it was an argument developed after the decision was made, and this argument was not the reason for the original decision.

In Britain the decision to develop its own nuclear arms was made in the 1940s, whereas the argument that it was necessary to have them for deterrence purposes dates from the 1950s. In 1950s Britain came the rise of CND and other opposition to nuclear arms, which had a particular effect on the Labour Party, and it was then that the Labour Party establishment came up with the justifications that they were necessary so long as we faced the nuclear arms of a totalitarian opponent. ('The very thing which makes it possible for people to demonstrate against nuclear arms is our own nuclear arms.')

The Conservatives too supported nuclear arms, which for them was more natural, but they equally joined in the deterrence argument when it was made.

But it's clear, and was explicit at the time, that the original decision was made on great power grounds, and the consideration that there was any particular adversary who had to be deterred was secondary. Even if there was such an adversary the determination to have nuclear weapons came first, and even if the adversary was to disappear that that would not cause them to abandon their nuclear weapons. Indeed, that is exactly what was to happen in the period between Gorbachev and Putin.

Still, the argument that nuclear weapons were an unfortunate necessity for the time being, so long as there was this other side which also had nuclear weapons, was presented and taken seriously even by the people who presented it. It lifted off into a policy prescription in its own right and became the doctrine of Mutually Assured Deterrence, gleefully acronymed as MAD. As early as 1960, in John Kennedy's campaign for the American presidency, he emphasised the alleged 'missile gap' with the Soviet Union, and under his presidency American nuclear arms, with Soviet nuclear arms following suit, were expanded to numbers sufficient to eliminate everything on earth several times over.

In Britain the Conservatives were happy with a mixture of the nuclear-weapons-for-deterrence doctrine and nuclear-weapons-for-great-power-status doctrine, with little recognition that these were even different. For Labour the situation was trickier, for the instinct of the typical party member was more likely to be visions of world peace than visions of British greatness.

First Aldermaston march against nuclear weapons sets off, 1958 (: Past Tense[1])

---

[1] First Today in London radical history: first Aldermaston march against nuclear weapons sets off, 1958, *Past Tense*, 4th April, https://pasttenseblog.wordpress.com/2016/04/04/first-today-in-london-radical-history-first-aldermaston-march-against-nuclear-weapons-sets-off-1958/

The Campaign for Nuclear Disarmament, famous everywhere just by its initials CND and its line-and-two-legs logo, quickly obtained enormous following in the Labour Party, and consequent pressure was put on an unwilling leadership to at least make moves in the direction of its political demands.

The demands of CND were not actually all that clear, except that they wanted somehow to be rid of nuclear weapons. This became known as 'unilateralism' because they wanted Britain to get rid of its nuclear weapons irrespective of what other countries did. As for the political consequences of such a move, the demand was made for Britain to abandon its close association with America in confrontation with the Soviet Union and become a neutral country ('neutralism'), like Sweden and Switzerland during the two world wars, and most third world countries and ex-colonies opted for after independence.

Ideas like that were regarded by the mainstream politicians, the Labour leadership as much as the Conservatives, with about as much enthusiasm as the 17th century church reacting to the ideas of Galileo. The American alliance was central in their outlook about where Britain was in the world and what it was stood for. It hadn't reached the extraordinary lengths it has now, but identification with America was already vehement.

But Labour, at least, had to take CND seriously, or at least a serious challenge to their previous policies, so the claim was made that what the 'moderate leadership' believed in was multilateral, as opposed to unilateral, nuclear disarmament. If only and when the international situation came to permit it, they would be the first at the conference tables offering negotiations towards the eventual elimination of nuclear weapons (they said this with straight faces), though provided it was by everyone, for sure themselves included.

When Labour next came to power with the Wilson government elected in 1964, the insincerity of the claim became undeniable. In the election campaign Harold Wilson had spoken vaguely of subsuming Britain's independent nuclear weapons into a general western deterrent, but absolutely nothing happened about that. Wilson's own technique was to simply refuse to discuss the matter, and he got away with it. He simply brushed questioning aside on the matter, confident that so long as he was in power no serious effort would be made from inside his party to derail him on this matter.

And that situation continued. When in 2008-9 Gordon Brown's Labour government came under party pressure to give substance to their vague assurances that they remained committed to eventual international negotiations on the abolition of nuclear weapons, it tried to divert attention by pointing to some worthy but obscure negotiations for better control of fissile materials that Britain was engaged in at that very moment, negotiations that had been going on for years and may still be going on so far as anyone knows. Until a change of heart is brought about (somehow), both main parties (and the Liberal Democrats) intend Britain to stay armed with nuclear weapons for ever, no matter what else happens or doesn't happen in the world. Claims that they would like to stop nuclear proliferation are true but only relatively; they'd like to stop it for countries they disapprove of, but even then, not if the price is that they'd ever have to give up their own.

The menace from the east

An Historical Perspective of Russia (Source: Giffard[1])

There is a longstanding history of Russophobia in Europe. The very image of the country, larger than all other European countries put together, is enough to make it a menace in the eyes of those who see international relations as a contest for the strongest. Napoleon thought Russia a

---

[1] Giffard, L. (2018), 'The media coverage of Russophobia', *Institute for a Greater Europe*, 17th June, https://www.institutegreatereurope.com/single-post/2018/06/17/the-media-coverage-of-russophobia-and-the-current-diplomatic-crisis-between-russia-an

menace to his hegemony, and so did the Prussians. Even the British in the 19th century, who might have been the last to fear Russia, got locked in a contest with them for influence in India and south Asia (known with open cynicism as the 'Great Game'). In both world wars Russophobia was the very centrepiece of German propaganda – the brooding menace in the east, the country where travellers disappeared and dark unspeakable things happened, the enemy of the civilisation that had built up over the centuries in central and western Europe.

So, there's this response of fear and hostility towards a large country simply because it's there. It really does exist. But can that alone be enough to explain how the renewed hostility between the west and Russia came about? After all it might have been thought (and Hitler famously did think) that the rise of America to great power status would cause the Europeans to develop this attitude towards the United States; and in particular war was inevitable between Britain and the US for pre-eminence in the English-speaking world. Instead, we have the British mainstream attitude of enthusiasm for satellite status with the US, and though the British attitude is the most extreme, continental Europe has also welcomed the post-war American involvement in its affairs.

In addition to the historical attitudes of the west towards Russia, Russia in turn has a suspicion of the west. Historical scholars tend to emphasise the inbuilt wariness with which Russians view the west, if not indeed the whole world; it may sound as if the scholars are postulating an unreal degree of inherited memory, but the speeches of Russian politicians do bear them out, at least partially.

Even in Soviet times the speeches of Brezhnev and others about alleged ill-will toward Russia in the past was a noticeable feature of the official rhetoric. You might have supposed that this was merely propaganda, but as a 1960's writer on arms control observed, the thing to understand was that Brezhnev and co. really did think like that.[1] Even during the relatively short-lived period of reconciliation between Russia and the west this feature of the rhetoric was observed. At first the western foreign services considered it most unfortunate that the Russian Foreign Minister under Yeltsin continued to be Evgeny Primakov, for he had served during Soviet times and was considered to be instinctively anti-western. In time Primakov was succeeded by Kosyrev, and later by Lavrov, but it made no difference. Russian complaints about the west continued, and not just western behaviour at the time but over centuries past.

When most western foreign ministers make speeches, or write articles, there is usually a limit to how far into history they delve, even if they are delivering complaints about the behaviour of someone else. There is also, usually, a limit to any tone of personal bitterness about alleged historical wrongs. But the speeches and articles of Russian politicians are full of a narrative of national victimhood stretching back to the very origin of the Russian state. In a typical article for a foreign policy magazine in 2016 [2] the then-and-now

---

[1] Elizabeth Young, A Farewell to Arms Control, Penguin 1972

[2] https://archive.mid.ru/en/foreign_policy/news/-/asset_publisher/cKNonkJE02Bw/content/id/2124391

foreign minister Lavrov ranges over the foundation of the Russian state as Rus in (now) Ukraine in 988 AD, the Mongolian invasions some centuries later, allegations that from the start countries to the west tried to isolate it and stymie it, allegations that over the subsequent centuries the west tried to prevent Russia attaining its natural greatness, and so on and on. It is as if a British delegation negotiating with the French was to attack them angrily for the Norman Conquest or attack an Italian delegation for the Roman conquest.

It was in this culture that Nato insisted on a policy of expansion to take in the countries surrounding Russia but excluding Russia itself. And not just any countries but countries with bitterly anti-Russian governments, and not just bitterly anti-Russian governments but restive Russian minorities which in some cases had even been deprived of citizenship. And not only taking these countries in but sending troops there to 'deter' any Russian ideas about them, and not only sending troops but ostentatiously inviting the international media to witness large scale exercises.

On the other side, the allegation that the present Russian leaders want to abolish the dissolution of the Soviet Union also has some substance, at least in hegemonic terms. Putin's own opinions seem Russian nationalist though not communist, despite his deploring the ending of the Soviet Union. But speeches by Putin himself [1] as well as others

---

[1] see e.g. Putin's address to the Duma in 2014: http://en.kremlin.ru/events/president/news/20603

lament the dissolution and unmistakably take the view that the territories concerned are indeed within a rightful sphere of influence of Russia. None of this justifies the decision to expand Nato, and the larger message it contained about who now ruled the world, but there is truth in the allegations that Russia does not genuinely accept the independence of the former Soviet republics, or at least not their full independence.

In late 2021 the Russians sent troops into Kazakhstan to support its authoritarian government facing popular discontent, and there is no doubt about the Russian motive. The Kazakhstan government may be good or bad, but it is pro-Russian and is seen as keeping Kazakhstan (the largest of the ex-Soviet republics) within Russia's sphere of hegemony. The fact that Kazakhstan's government is only pseudo-democratic is no objection either, since the Russian government is not much more genuinely democratic itself. Authoritarians supporting one another has become an extra aspect of the situation since Yeltsin's capricious rule gave way to Putin's abused democracy.

Then in February of 2022 Russia invaded Ukraine, a situation which we have yet to see fully play out. Here the Russians have stated explicitly that their primary motivation is to stop Nato expansion, and to all but the most blinkered western hawk it clearly is, whatever you think of this method of doing it. But there is clearly this second aspect of considering Ukraine within the Russian sphere – indeed in the case of Ukraine, hardly a separate country at

---

all. In this nationalist viewpoint we see a clear mirror image of the western sphere-of-hegemony vision. The west started it with Nato expansion, but the Russian nationalists were only too ready to react in kind, and with the added dimension that they stand for dictatorship rather than democracy.

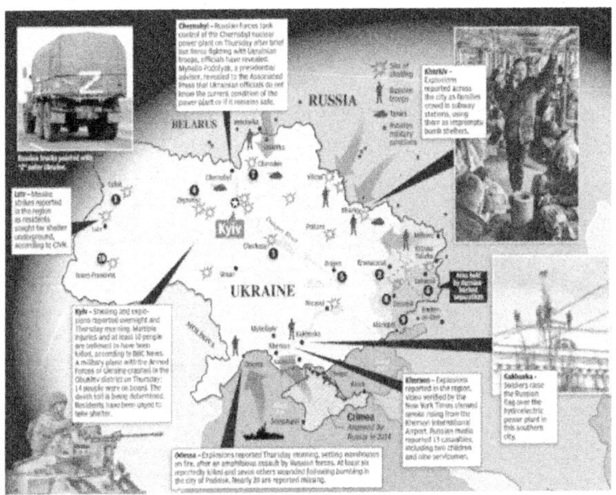

Russia Invades Ukraine (Source: Simko-Bednarski[1])

Armed democracy

Then there's the claim to the west's moral superiority because of our superior political system. And of course,

---

[1] Simko-Bednarski, E. (2022), 'Why is Russia invading Ukraine? Explaining the roots of a long-simmering conflict;, New York Post, 24th February, https://nypost.com/2022/02/24/why-is-russia-invading-ukraine-explaining-the-roots-of-a-long-simmering-conflict/

western democracy is genuinely better than the range of other systems around, from authoritarian pseudo-democracies to total dictatorships, to totalitarianism of the Soviet sort. Actually, the last of these is rare nowadays – there is only North Korea that readily comes to mind, since even China under Xi Jinping has retreated from the horrors of Maoism to the extent that ordinary Chinese people can even be interviewed in the street (usually), even though, of course, they cannot have any effect on the practices of their leaders.

The scope for self-righteousness in the west does have its limitations though. Public opinion in western democracies is open and free enough, and there is often pressure of public opinion which drives the actions of the politicians, but it rarely manifests itself on foreign policy issues. Even outright wars rarely have a decisive effect on public opinion, and when it does it's likely to be approving. The result is that the political classes are free enough in practice to follow their instincts when it comes to foreign and defence policy – and these instincts largely coincide between the mainstream politicians of whichever party. It has meant that the most powerful of the democracies have been fully as ready as the most powerful of the dictatorships to 'intervene' abroad, i.e., join in existing wars or even start wars, to occupy countries when they feel strongly so-inclined, or when they don't go that far to intervene behind the scenes in other countries by backing one side or another in internal power struggles, and so on.

The justifications given are that in immediate terms we must protect our interests, that we face non-democratic rivals who will intervene to their own advantage (and our disadvantage) if we don't intervene ourselves, and that in a larger sense we must protect our very existence as democracies from the evil forces that would destroy us. Some people may regard this as stating no more than the obvious, though others regard it as blinkered self-righteousness. Certainly, the implication that the dictatorships are out to destroy us as such is basically fantasy, though many of the dictatorships do have grievances against us and tend to act on those grievances, as in the case of Russia (and you could add China and Iran and many others).

The claim to moral superiority tends to co-exist, often in the same human individuals, with the 'rivals for hegemony' view of the world, that international relations are really about the struggle for supremacy between the largest powers and blocs, itself an amoral process irrespective of ideological differences or any other differences when it really comes down to it. Any apparent contradiction is dismissed by pointing out that it so happens that in our case the timeless struggle for supremacy with others coincides with ourselves being the better people with the better system and a better pattern of behaviour, so we can be doubly confident about the ethic as well as necessity of the struggle. But it's a timeless struggle, for we will always have to fight for dominance against the challengers. This outlook on the world, the same as the outlook which is mainstream among the Nato secretariat, is evidently satisfactory to its exponents, even a personally satisfying view of the world in which they want to live. It is a measure of how very much the wrong people are still dominant in the decision-making apparatus in the west.

Chapter 4

The Leibowitz syndrome

In the 1950s there was a popular science fiction novel, 'A Canticle for Leibowitz',[1] which was evidently an allegory about the chronic flaw in human nature that led to endless cycles of new wars. Set in a monastery after a nuclear catastrophe, we watch through the eyes of the monks as the human race outside their walls rebuilds through a long period of thousands of years – and then, with the technology and abilities back in place, moves irresistibly to another nuclear catastrophe.

The novel had a religious denouement, though you don't have to accept that to get the point. In real life nuclear catastrophe hasn't happened (yet), though there were several near misses during the cold war. Then suddenly the threat seemed to lift with the coming to power of communist reformers in the Soviet Union, and then non-communist democracy in Russia. But now we are back to the nuclear stand-off.

The other difference of course is that in real life it hasn't taken thousands of years to get back to the same situation. The world's leaders have managed it in thirty.

---

[1] Walter M. Miller Jnr., A Canticle for Leibowitz, 1960.

Putin arrives

Yeltsin Selects His Successor (Source: BBC[1])

As the twentieth century came to an end, in Russia the ailing Yeltsin made repeated attempts to find a suitable successor to himself. In 1999 he finally chose Vladimir Putin, an ex-KGB officer, and who was to show himself to have, thoroughly, the attributes to be expected of a former member of the security services.

It is remarkable how what was to come was expected from the start, in selecting an ex-spook for head of state. It was even said at the time that his demeanour 'frightened the

[1] Rosenberg, S. (2014), Have 15 years of power gone to Putin's head?, *BBC News*, 31st December, https://www.bbc.co.uk/news/world-europe-30533034

children.' But although the reaction to Putin was distinctly cool in the west, it also seemed to accept the inevitability of a more authoritarian and perhaps Russian nationalist regime, after the way Yeltsin had substituted chaos for democracy in post-communist Russia.

For sure Putin technically had to be elected, but in a sign of what was to come this was already a done deal. Yeltsin wanted to hand over his power and the power of his family to someone suitable (and, it's alleged, obtain his family's immunity from future prosecution for the way they had behaved during his period of power), and after several aborted attempts he found Putin.

The general trend under Putin is well known. The independence of newspapers and television channels ended, bringing them into thinly disguised state control. Elections continued, but with heavy rigging. Opinions differ as to how much difference the rigging made however, since from the start Putin seems to have had the support of most Russians.

This was particularly so when it came to the so-called oligarchs, the businessmen who had grown massively rich during Russia's brief but spectacular period of privatisation of the state-owned businesses, in particular by obtaining control over the natural resources that were the country's principal source of wealth.

Putin's Personal Enrichment (Source: Podkopaev[1])

The perception was that they were crooks on a massive scale, and deserved, at very least, to be brought sharply to heel. They had established themselves under Yeltsin, and the situation was not totally discontinued under Putin, but they had to come to terms with the fact that they were under a less tolerant regime. Of course, this lesser tolerance was most shown if they tried any form of political opposition. Most people in the west have heard names like Gusinsky, Berezovsky and Khodorkovsky who had to flee Russia or were imprisoned there, and it's impossible to say what mixture was involved of business illegality and political expediency. Oligarchs who came to terms with the regime did well however, generally making personal connections with members of Putin's team or even his family.

---

[1] Podkopaev, P. (2016), 'Comrade Moneybags: How Much is Putin Worth?', Hudson Institute, 16th December, https://www.hudson.org/research/13172-comrade-moneybags-how-much-is-putin-worth

One of the first situations which Putin's regime faced was Chechen separatism. Although the Soviet Union had been ended by Yeltsin, Russia itself was a federation and there were separatist movements in the fringe members. In particular the Caucasian region of Chechnya wanted to imitate the success of the ex-Soviet but non-Russian republics and obtain independence, and there was an uprising in progress in the last years of Yeltsin's rule. Putin suppressed it with military force, and there were reports of brutality in doing so which led to great unfavourable publicity outside Russia, particularly in the west. There had been wariness from the start of Putin's rule; now there were human rights criticisms, and this got West-Putin relations off to a cool start.

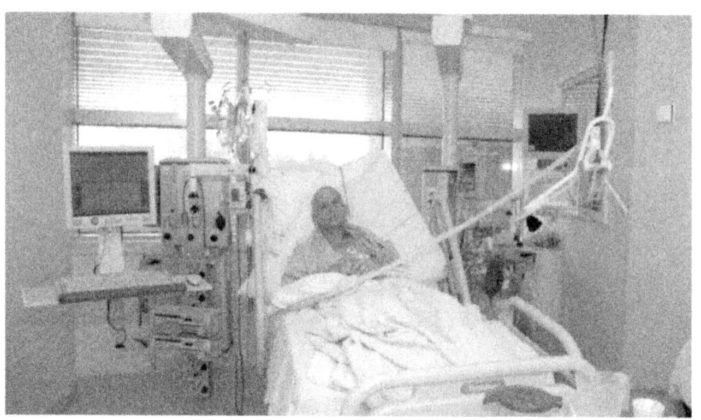

Ex-Russian Spy Alexander Litvinenko in Intensive Care Unit of University College Hospital November 20th, 2006

(Source: Natasja Weitsz/Getty Images)

Other acts of the ex-spook Putin had severe repercussions for his image in the west: he assassinated people. And not just on Russian territory, but even targets who had left the country and taken (or tried to take) refuge abroad. The well-known cases in Britain were defectors from the Russian secret service: Alexander Litvinenko, who was poisoned by polonium (a radioactive substance) in London in 2006, and the father and daughter Sergei and Yulia Skripal in Salisbury in 2018. There is no dispute that the targets were former Russian agents who, from the Russian point of view, had turned traitor. But there are tacit rules of the game even in spying, and assassinations on foreign territory are outside them. To some extent the matter goes beyond Putin into the whole culture of the Russian secret services, and their difference from the western ones.

All sides spy on everyone else of course. But western spies know that if they are caught, they are likely to suffer the consequences, and unlikely to be rescued by their own side; rather their own side will simply issue the standard denials and leave them to their fate. Not always of course, for spy exchanges are famous in history; but usually. But the Russian secret service, and before that the Soviet secret service, was famously loyal to their own people provided those people remained loyal to them and would go to almost any lengths to rescue their operatives if they got into trouble.

This may seem rather admirable, but the other side of it is that if any of their operatives turned traitor, they would go to almost any lengths to make them pay the price. And that is what they set out to do in these cases. But even given the culture, Putin was going further in assassinating defectors on foreign territory and doing it so brazenly.

Governments react very strongly to assassinations on their territory, as Putin would have known. Yet he did it.

Putin is the sort of leader for whom it's easy for outsiders to adopt an attitude of moralistic antagonism. Yet the main thing which Putin set out to be antagonistic to the west about was Nato expansion, and the Russian attitude to Nato expansion was not invented by Putin and is very unlikely to have been different without Putin.

The neocons

Meanwhile in America, at the turn of the century it was becoming clear that there was a large, growing and influential group on the militaristic right who were simply drunk with a sense of American power, and out for the political and personal satisfaction of seeing that power used.

These were the people who took literally the rhetoric about the west having won the Cold War, and for them this was an opportunity to be seized – and no nonsense about the opportunity being for any new international order, but for American world domination. Taking the terminology from economists who referred to the growingly interconnected world as neo-liberalism, this group on the American right became known as the neo-conservatives, neocons for short.

Key Neoconservatives, secretary of defense Donald Rumsfeld, President George W. Bush and vice-president Dick Cheney (Source: Zuesse[1])

They soon had a think tank associated with them, and its name became famous: 'Project for the New American Century'. Its preliminary 'Statement of Principles' when it was set up in 1997 has become famous[2]. Near the beginning it goes:

As the 20th century draws to a close, the United States stands as the world's preeminent power. Having led the West to victory in the Cold War, America faces an opportunity and

---

[1] Zuesse, E. (2018), 'Neocons hate Russia even more than they hate any other nation', *Modern diplomacy*, 31st July, https://moderndiplomacy.eu/2018/07/31/neocons-hate-russia-even-more-than-they-hate-any-other-nation/

[2] https://web.archive.org/web/20050205041635/http://www.newamericancentury.org/statementofprinciples.htm

a challenge: Does the United States have the vision to build upon the achievements of past decades? Does the United States have the resolve to shape a new century favorable to American principles and interests?

We are in danger of squandering the opportunity and failing the challenge. We are living off the capital -- both the military investments and the foreign policy achievements -- built up by past administrations...

We seem to have forgotten the essential elements of the Reagan Administration's success: a military that is strong and ready to meet both present and future challenges; a foreign policy that boldly and purposefully promotes American principles abroad; and national leadership that accepts the United States' global responsibilities.

The neocons couldn't have hoped for a better outcome than they got in the 2000 presidential election. George W. Bush had campaigned on a vague platform of 'compassionate conservatism', but as soon as elected he showed instincts that were fully in accord with the neocons. He brought with him a team of fierce conservatives who had long considered that the US had been led for too many years by effete liberals who had allowed the country to be kicked around; now they were going to damned well put things right. Almost immediately they announced that the US would withdraw from a number of international treaties, including the Anti-Ballistic Missile treaty, and the Kyoto protocol, a treaty to limit the emission of greenhouse gases. And as one commentator said, the announcement of their intentions was done in an unmistakably in-your-face manner, making clear the emotions of the Bush team in spitting bile at the loathsome liberals.

Russia was not the main focus of the Bush administration's attention; if anything their attitude was that since Russia was knocked out as a competitor for world domination, at least for a while, they should search around for new enemies in place of old, and in early 2001 had settled on deliberately winding up the Chinese (following an incident in which an American and a Chinese aircraft collided in the air, and the American crew were detained for a while on a Chinese island) when 9/11 intervened. Suddenly they had an excellent new enemy, which they made the very most of. This was the chance to show the world, not only what happened if anyone 'messed with us,' but their awesome military might, and that it was America who now ruled the world after the end of communism.

Subsequent events in Afghanistan and then Iraq are well known. As far as Russia was concerned the priority of the Bush administration was a renewed determination to push ahead with Missile Defense (i.e. the anti-missile missile programme, still on and off the agenda since talks between Reagan and Gorbachev had broken down). Clinton had not discontinued it but hadn't pushed it much further ahead, seeming to be in two minds about it, but his successor Bush had no such hesitation. Russian objections were merely a further attraction, since it allowed them to emphasise where power now lay in the world. When Condoleeza Rice (Bush's National Security Advisor, later his Secretary of State) was asked why, if missile defense was purely defensive and not directed against any particular state, they were so determined to site the bases in the countries round Russia, she answered that Russia was not entitled to dictate what happened in any other country.

This answer, which on the face of it very obviously isn't an answer to the question, yet just beneath the surface does answer by virtue of the attitude it advertises, has been adopted in the years since as the answer why Nato has a God-given right to expand wherever and whenever it pleases, particularly in the countries around Russia.

It is worth remarking, too, that though the Bush administration was unpopular even with the orthodox elites abroad, the criticism was not of its world view (which basically was shared by the Democrats in America and the top officials in Nato headquarters) but of its unilateralism in acting without consultation with the people who considered themselves allies and were merely annoyed by the reminder of their secondary status.

The rise of the hawks

With the emergence of Putin in Russia there was also an emergence, or re-emergence, in the west of hard-liners towards Russia. Some had never really gone away, such as the advocates of Nato expansion for whom the end of Soviet communism was no reason to end hostility towards Russia. Still there were new individuals in the west, both among politicians and journalists, who made it their trademark to be warning the public of the new menace from the east. This menace was to be watched for and acted against. What exactly the action was that they wanted was not completely specified, but there was no mistaking the warlike tone with which they expressed themselves.

One name which became well known in Britain was Edward Lucas, a mildly spoken journalist, and son of an Oxford philosopher who was known for claiming that a famous result in mathematics called Gödel's theorem contained a message about the nature of human consciousness. His son's interests are less theoretical and more full-bloodied. Described by the Center for European Policy Analysis (CEPA) as 'an internationally recognized expert on espionage, subversion, the use and abuse of history, energy security and information warfare' (and presumably anything else which appeals to paranoia), he has been a foreign correspondent of various media outlets since the 1990s and has been pushing for conflict with Russia as hard as he can, at every opportunity, since the mid 2000s. So far as we know he has never actually said he wants World War 3, but it's hard to see what else he wants. Here is his inspiring address to his constituency, quoted from a webpage announcing his prospective parliamentary candidature on behalf of the Liberal Democrats (yes, the Liberal Democrats) for the Cities of London and Westminster[1].

> *For years I have tried to influence the course of events through writing and speaking. I've had some success — back in 2008 my book The New Cold War helped wake up opinion in the West to the danger posed by Putin's Kremlin. Deception,*

---

[1] https://www.markpack.org.uk/168013/edward-lucas-selected-in-cities-of-london-and-westminster/

a few years later, did the same for what we now call "hybrid warfare". I've done a lot on China, too. I wrote countless articles for the Times and Economist, and my weekly column for CEPA, as well as think-tank studies.

But we're losing. So instead standing on the sidelines urging politicians to do things, I've decided to get stuck in.

My aim is simple: to save democracy from dirty money, disinformation and digital manipulation. We in the UK take our institutions, freedom and rule of law for granted. That's a mistake. They're under threat. We need to defend them

The central London constituency I have chosen exemplifies much of what is best and worst about Britain. It's home to the beating heart of our democracy. It's also home to the cesspit that poisons it — the pinstriped traitors who launder money and reputations, corrode public trust and peddle influence in our politics.

Another ultra-hawk who has become a familiar figure in the British media is Anne Applebaum, a harsh-voiced American writer of even harsher opinions. She can lay claim to be a more heavyweight figure who has held academic posts and written books, mostly on the worst excesses of the Soviet system. She has also been a member of various right-wing think-tanks and is married to the former Polish foreign minister Radoslaw Sikorski. Among other things she is one of the originators of the line that Russian objection to Nato expansion are merely cover for fear of democracy on its doorstep, and hence all the more reason for Nato to press harder on Russia's borders. In 2016 she urged Ukraine and other east European countries to prepare for 'total war' with Russia, dismissed scornfully 'the myth of Russian humiliation', and described Nato expansion as a 'phenomenal success.' Like Edward Lucas she puts a lot of emphasis on alleged covert Russian manipulation of the media, false propaganda, fake news and so on, the evil that is around us everywhere, yet most of us, us fools, don't see it.

You could dismiss two particular people as merely a lunatic fringe, not representative of mainstream opinion. But since the coming of Putin, they have been planting their seeds into ever more fertile soil. Putin's annexation of Crimea was a godsend to them, and recent events in Ukraine the ultimate godsend. Despite her strongly right-wing opinions Anne Applebaum supported Hillary Clinton in the 2016 American presidential election, because she was the more hostile to Russia, and indeed Hillary Clinton was known to be looking forward to an early confrontation with Russia in Syria. But then, Hillary Clinton is testament to the fact that belief that an assertive American foreign policy is not the preserve of the Republican party but is shared by plenty of Democrats. When Clinton was beaten by Trump, it immediately started being put about by 'her team' that she had been robbed of the presidency by Russia – i.e. covert Russian cyber manipulation – with heavy hints that Trump himself was a Russian stooge or even an outright secret agent of Russia, and this has been doctrine ever since among muscular liberals in America.

As the years passed and outright hostility developed between Russia and the west, the western hawks have come to dominate the narrative to an alarming extent. Rory Stewart, claimed to be something of the Conservative Party's resident intellectual, said on television during his period as chair of the Defence Select Committee, that with Russia we faced an enemy that was exploring ceaselessly how far it could go and get away with things, probing our every weakness, seeing what our strengths were, probing endlessly till we show what we're made of.[1] This mixture of playground machismo and paranoia has become the normal tone of western commentary at the time of writing. It is surprising that in the age when all sides concerned have nuclear weapons anyone should actually push for war with Russia, but since Putin got going that is what the western hawks are doing.

Putin gets going

Actually, most of the things which people presently associate with Putin had already got going when he arrived on the scene. Russian anger at Nato expansion was being thoroughly aired (and dismissed with sneering contempt by Nato protagonists). The chaos in the ex-Soviet republics surrounding Russia had also got going. The clash of

[1] We do not have an exact transcript, but we are definitely not misrepresenting him.

nationalisms in disputed areas which had been the thing which even the Soviet Union with all its powers of suppression had found hard to deal with, immediately came right out into the open again. In the Baltic states, which were in the first tranche of ex-Soviet entrants to Nato, there were substantial Russian minorities, mostly people who had settled during the Soviet period, and now faced public resentment towards them. Simultaneously their governments are vehemently anti-Russian, were the first of the ex-Soviet republics to join Nato, and in Nato are among the most aggressive in pushing for further Nato expansion. Two of the three Baltic states have deprived the Russian minorities of citizenship, with laws which only gave citizenship to pre-Soviet citizens and their descendants. The Russian minorities have not been expelled, but they remain where they are as stateless people. They can apply for naturalisation, but among other things have to take a test of the local Baltic language, which of course the Russians tend to fail. In Latvia where the Russian speakers are a quarter of the population, they were able under the constitution to obtain a referendum which sought to make Russian a recognised second language, but this was heavily defeated by the Latvian majority. There are clearly no good feelings towards or by the Russian minorities in the Baltic states.

In other areas fighting broke out even as the Soviet Union was ending, especially in the Caucasus. The case of Armenia and Azerbaijan, fighting over an Armenian populated area inside Azerbaijan, is well known. There have already been two wars here, the first of which began in 1988 when they were still both supposed to be part of the Soviet Union. Armenia won the first war, and incorporated the enclave into its territory, but there was another war in 2020 which Azerbaijan won. In this case Russia has come out as a champion of Armenia, and as ever the reasons have less to do with the legacy of the Soviet Union than factors which stretch back into history. Armenia had been a Christian entity in a Muslim area, and as such cherished by imperial Russia for centuries. It is alleged by Azerbaijan that Russian help for Armenia is the reason Armenia won the first war (though if true it makes it surprising that Armenia lost the second time).

Particularly significant, because of the precedent it set, was Georgia and its two breakaway regions of Abkhazia and South Ossetia. Again, the reasons go back into pre-Soviet history and not all the inhabitants of the areas concerned felt themselves to be a separate nationality to Georgian. But enough did for there to be immediate rebellion after Georgian independence when the Soviet Union was dissolved in 1991.

The year 2008 is a key year, for that was when Putin set his precedent. After years of an uneasy truce in which Abkhazia and South Ossetia were *de facto* independent of Georgia, and protected by Russia, the president of Georgia made a sudden attempt to solve the problem by force, sending in his troops to crush the secession. Putin responded by sending in his own troops and expelling the Georgian troops, and ever since then these two enclaves have been independent (in theory; in practice protectorates of Russia), and Putin has demonstrated that once he has taken small breakaway states under his wing, he will protect them – at least in the ex-Soviet region, and against pro-western other states.

Abkhazia and South Ossetia (Source: Economist[1])

The egregious case, now dominating the headlines, is Ukraine. The background is a complicated story, hard for those not on the ground to follow. Ukraine is a split state, with areas in the east and south where the people speak Russian whereas in the west people speak a distinctive Ukrainian language. It used to be said that the Russian speakers in the east regarded themselves as Russians, but this has been denied by some commentators since the invasion of Ukraine. But it is definitely the case that splits

---

[1] Economist (2008), 'South Ossetia is not Kosovo', *Economist Leader*, 30th August, https://www.economist.com/leaders/2008/08/28/south-ossetia-is-not-kosovo

between the Russian speakers in the east and Ukrainian speakers in the west have played a major part in the political instability of Ukraine in the last 30 years. Into the bargain Ukraine suffered from an almost hopeless economic situation, and it was notorious for severe corruption in almost every part of life.

An attempt was made at first to run it as a united state, but lack of trust everywhere had its effect. In 2004 the presidential election was won by a Russian speaking and pro-Russian candidate from the east, Victor Yanucovych, but there were claims of widespread rigging, leading to massive protests in the capital Kiev (itself in the west of Ukraine). The protests became so severe that the result was annulled, and Yanucovych's Ukrainian-speaking rival Yuschenko was declared elected. These events became known as the 'Orange Revolution' or 'Colour Revolution' and were massively resented by the Russian Ukrainians and also by Russia itself, which regarded it as a takeover by the west.

But then in 2010 the Russian-Ukrainian Yanucovych succeeded in a second bid for the presidency, after an election which was internationally witnessed and accepted. He then proceeded to rule as if determined to justify all previous fears about him. An example which became internationally famous was the imprisonment of the prime minister in a previous government, Yulia Tymoshenko, for alleged abuse of power and embezzlement, the grounds being that a deal she made with the Russian gas company Gazprom for supply of gas was unsatisfactory and should have been much better. Unsurprisingly this attracted not only anger inside Ukraine but international condemnation;

however, Yanucovych remained obdurate and Tymoshenko remained in prison for three years until released by the overthrow of Yanucovych (for a second time) in 2013.

This was again brought about by the conflicting wishes of Ukrainian nationalists and Russian Ukrainians about whether the country should lean towards Russia or the west. An agreement had been made between previous governments of Ukraine and the European Union for a trade deal, but Yanucovych refused to sign it, and wanted a trade deal with Russia instead. There were massive protests in Kiev, which turned violent and became another uprising, known as the 'Maidan revolution' (after the central square in Kiev), or 'Revolution of Dignity'. Eventually an agreement was made between Yanucovych and the opposition parties in parliament for an interim government and early elections, but this didn't last. After more violence in Kiev Yanucovych was forced to flee the country. An interim government took over which then signed the agreement with the EC.

Russia believed this second overthrow of a pro-Russian leader to be a western-plotted coup to snatch Ukraine from the Russian sphere of influence into a western one. In fact, there does not appear to be any evidence that anyone in the west was directly behind the violence, certainly not in the sense of having specifically plotted it, though the western governments did support the interim government which followed. But the Russians, and Putin specifically, believed it was a western plot, and reacted with violence of their own.

Russia Invades and Annexes Crimea (Source: Walker, Salem and MacAskill[1])

Putin's response was the worst and most self-parodying you would expect a leader of his type. He invaded and annexed a slice of Ukrainian territory, namely Crimea. Even given his belief about the Maidan revolution, how he thought that this was an appropriate response is very hard to understand. It is true that Crimea is largely Russian in population and was part of Russia until Khrushchev in 1954 transferred it to Crimea as a purely administrative act within the Soviet Union, and Russia might even have made a claim on Ukraine about it. But for the larger country to suddenly seize it by force from the smaller country was not the way to pursue the claim, with the reminder of Hitler that is inevitable. An added bitter irony is that Ukraine had been

[1] Walker, S., Salem, H. and MacAskill, E. (2014), 'Russian 'invasion' of Crimea fuels fear of Ukraine conflict', *Guardian*, 1st March, https://www.theguardian.com/world/2014/feb/28/russia-crimea-white-house

one of the two countries (the other was South Africa) to inherit a nuclear weapons programme, but to eschew it, a rare example to the world of a willingness to contribute to nuclear disarmament. And this was its reward.

After Crimea

Crimea gave the western hawks everything they could have dreamed of. Those who'd always wanted renewed confrontation with Russia were in their element. The western hegemonists (whose outlook was now mirrored by Putin) could, and did, present Nato expansion as a protection needed by all against the evil Putin – and further afield, against China and anyone else handy.

Nato expansion was now the central western policy, and not only against Russia. The policy was that whenever there was a conflict situation which western countries got involved in, Nato requested to take over, and was usually granted its wish. Even in the First Gulf War it played a heavy supporting role in Turkey, and after that it always set out to get directly involved. When the Bosnian War broke out in the Balkans a 'No Fly Zone' was eventually established by the UN Security Council, and it looked at first as if any international action would be under UN auspices. But the dominant western powers in the intervention handed the matter over to Nato, to the disconcertion and displeasure of the Russians (under Yeltsin at that time). Nato again took over in the Balkans when it was decided to intervene against Serbia's crackdown on Kosovo's separatists, to the further anger of Yeltsin's Russia, which considered itself still close to Serbia – nearly a century after Russia had last considered itself a protector of Serbia, again emphasising the longstandingness of some of the attitudes involved.

When the Bush administration was succeeded by Obama, he famously stated in his accession speech that he wanted to 'reset' the relationship with Russia, and also added a few vague words about wanting to eliminate all nuclear weapons one day, words that caused a swooning Nobel committee to immediately award him the Nobel Peace Prize. (Though how seriously Obama meant it was shown by his adding in the same sentence that he didn't expect to see it in his lifetime.) He made a few minimal alterations to the policies which were winding up the Russians and drew back from the siting of missile defense bases in countries surrounding Russia, substituting warship-based missiles instead. But that was soon superseded, for Nato then successfully bid to take over the missile defense programme, and it restored land-based missiles.

We have written almost exclusively about relations with Russia so far, because that has been the most outstanding resurrection of world tension, but with the genie uncorked Nato expansion took place wherever and whenever Nato saw an opportunity. When the Arab Spring broke out in 2010-12, and when the Libyan dictator Gaddafi tried to crush it in his own country, the west was able to persuade enough other countries, including Russia, to support intervention to enable a UN Security Council mandate to declare a No-Fly Zone. But it wasn't really an international effort but from the start was the west out to overthrow Gaddafi. And very soon Nato bid to take it over, and did so, leaving Russia among others complaining that they'd been conned into giving approval to an apparently UN mission which had been a covert Nato intention from the start.

Putin made sure not to repeat the mistake in Syria. When the Syrian civil war got going against the Assad regime, the west equally wanted to intervene and overthrow a ruthless long-standing dictatorship which into the bargain (just coincidentally) had always been virulently anti-western. But Russia (and others) wasn't going to let the necessary Security Council resolution get through this time to give it the internationalist fig-leaf as had happened in Libya. More, Russia intervened itself, unilaterally, on behalf of Assad, treating him as a regional ally. This infuriated the west, not only because of such a choice of ally, but because of the very act of intervening in conflicts outside his own territory, which was the west's prerogative; and of course, he was also preventing Nato from taking over yet another western military action and hindering Nato expansion generally. Anywhere in the world where Nato sees an actual or nascent military conflict and it has influence with any of the parties involved, Nato takes the chance to 'give Nato a role' (a favourite phrase dating from the 1990s) and involves itself. While no individual western country is being directly expansionist (at least not in the old-fashioned sense of expanding its own territory) they are part of a collective organisation which is intensely expansionist on a global scale and constitutes the instrument of a hegemonist block.

However, for all Nato's aspirations to expand into the neighbours of Russia, it did appear that Russia had successfully deterred them from doing so in the cases of Ukraine or Georgia. It was a dismaying surprise when Putin suddenly massed troops on the Ukrainian border in early

2022 and announced that he would only move them away in exchange for an explicit guarantee that Ukraine would never join Nato, and more, that Nato would cease all further expansion in any areas around Russia, and more, that it would remove all military hardware from countries (members of Nato or not) which bordered Russia. These uncompromising demands, uncompromisingly worded, couldn't be intended to be acceptable to the west even as opening gambits in an intended negotiation. Not that the west showed the slightest willingness to compromise either – Nato expansion (now dignified under the name of its 'open door' policy) has become unquestionable doctrine. The most obvious conclusion is that Putin, for whatever reason (perhaps some internal political reason), was determined to be seen to have forced a public climbdown by the west of the sort that hardly a political leader in history would be willing to do, given the humiliating loss of political credibility. But since he must have known how unlikely that was, these demands must have been intended to be rejected, and to be used as a justification for invasion. And so he invaded, and once again has given the western hawks everything they dreamed of.

And so, in Leibowitz style we are back in the situation of armed standoff of the sort seen in the Cuban missile crisis of 1962, a standoff in which both sides have nuclear weapons. Inside Britain and other western countries, the ultra hawks, gagging for war, are making the running in the media, and have largely captured the narrative among the politicians. They are even referring to the Cuban missile crisis as the precedent to be followed. Truly, as Talleyrand famously said about the pre-revolution French monarchy, they have learnt nothing and forgotten nothing.

Chapter 5

An Alternative for Britain

Source: Nato[1]

We have made it clear that we regard Nato expansion as the long-term villain of the story, bound to lead eventually to a major clash with someone somewhere. It might not have been Russia, since Nato searches the world restlessly for conflicts anywhere Nato can 'find a role.' And the role is not like UN-style peacekeeping which, though armed, is usually neutral between the sides concerned and seeks to interpose

1 https://www.nato.int/cps/en/natohq/topics_81136.htm?selectedLocale=uk

itself between them. Nato by contrast seeks to choose a side and wage a war on behalf of that side.

But denouncing Nato expansion is not enough. Nato expansion is itself the result of a wrong attitude to global politics: that what the world must always be about is endless struggle for supremacy among the most powerful, with lesser powers choosing their sides and engaging in appropriate – though eventually shifting – alliances. Ironically Russia is accused of having exactly this attitude for invading Ukraine – more specifically that Russia is seeking a sphere of hegemony. But Nato expansion is the same attitude and applied on a whole world scale. This is not the time to argue about parallels, or alleged parallels, between present Russian behaviour and past and present western behaviour; rather we should say how we advocate those present policies be changed, and changed to what, how to move towards reconciliation with Russia (and other countries such as China and Iran), and what sort of world regime we should aspire to. This applies to the west as a whole, but we write more specifically about Britain, and the role Britain can play as a major western country in leading in a new direction.

A cooling down

Rather obviously, before there can be any reconciliation between Russia and the west there will have to be a (probably lengthy) period of cooling-down. As a member of Nato Britain is in a position to help – and this illustrates why, even in the unlikely event of a present-day British government being so minded, we are not advocating that Britain should leave Nato. Britain should stay in Nato and help reform it from within. Even at the moment Britain is a relative moderate inside the alliance (the hard liners inside Nato are the Russophobic eastern members plus the Nato secretariat) and if Britain associated itself with Nato reform it would find followers. Most west Europeans have little enthusiasm for confrontation with Russia and are only half hearted about the whole attitude of Nato taking over more and more of the world on behalf of the west.

Support for Nato militancy is still largely confined to enthusiasts below government level; it is worth noting that when during the build-up to the invasion of Ukraine various ultras demanded that Nato troops be sent there without delay and that Putin would then back down and run away with his tail between his legs, the governments of Britain and other key countries had enough sense to ignore them. In the short-term, all the British government can do is nod agreement about the wickedness of Putin, which is perfectly justifiable after all, implement economic sanctions, which damage us as well as Russia, but there you are, and quietly contribute whenever situation emerges.

In the medium-term we would hope that a reformist movement inside Nato can get going. There is the question of what we should advocate that Nato eventually becomes, but in a way, this is a relatively secondary matter: perhaps some regional grouping under UN auspices, but that can be discussed when the time comes. The effect simply of there being a reform in progress with the aim of Nato ceasing to be a confrontational block ever eagerly looking for wars to participate in, expand, and participate in still more wars, would be what is important. If and when things are back to relative normal (meaning some sort of truce in Ukraine at least) then it will be time for Britain to start showing a new orientation in its international profile.

A peacenik country

We would like Britain to gradually move its international positioning from membership of military pacts, plus enthusiastic satellite state of the USA, towards being part of – and hopefully a leading part of – a conciliation and peace grouping that centres its attention on the UN. One reaction to this suggestion may be that it sounds like the traditional image of Sweden or Switzerland, but it is not. These traditionally neutral countries put their emphasis not on contributing to the creation of international order but simply keeping out of any quarrel outside their own territories, regarding everything and anything as nothing to do with them, Nazism, Communism, the lot. At the same time, they maintained large citizen armies, to demonstrate that if anybody actually did invade them, they would have a fight on their hands. But we see Britain's future not in small-minded isolationism, but as a leading member of a world community working towards a genuine world order.

Another comparison which this might be reminiscent of, but not validly, is the so-called non-aligned grouping at the UN, which much was heard of during the cold war. But for a start, their so-called non-alignment had a strongly anti-western tint to it, which is hardly likely to commend it to most of British opinion. In fact, the very title non-aligned seemed to be taken most keenly by third-world countries which were strongly aligned towards the Soviet Union, and very many indeed of the countries which called themselves non-aligned were dictatorships. The terminology of non-alignment still exists, indeed it continued to be used even in the 1990s when there were the least reasons to detect power blocs to be aligned or not aligned to. So far as anyone tried to explain the meaning of non-alignment it was that non-aligned countries did not accept the division of the world into Communist and non-Communist blocs, but that is meaningless now.

But there are plenty of countries at the UN which have always been non-aligned in the literal sense and are genuinely interested in making moves towards international law and order. They even make periodic, and so far, doomed, efforts to advance the cause of multilateral nuclear disarmament. They can be expected to welcome a traditionally major power joining their concerns and wishing to be part of their efforts, provided the temptation is resisted to get carried away by this tradition and seek to be the immediate leader, which would obviously be resented.

In the aftermath of a period of renewed intense divisions among the major powers, which though started by Nato were joined in only too eagerly by Russia and also China, there would have to be the setting up of conciliation forums with which the 5 major powers would be engaged full time. Of course, there are plenty of conciliation forums already in the UN, and others which the UN is able to create when necessary, but a drive to end the situation which has developed would probably create some new ones. This would not only keep the sober-suited professional international diplomats usefully engaged in semi-permanent session but more seriously have the advantage that it would be subject to publicity which would in turn motivate it to actually reaching conclusions.

While the slow work is in progress of strengthening world order, centred on the UN which for all its imperfections is the only world body which is accepted as legitimate by most nations, Britain should start the military part of its reorientation by making more troops available for UN peace-keeping missions and less enthusiasm for Nato war-making ones. It should become more the norm for Britain to be contributing troops in UN enforcement roles, and less for Britain to be taking part in Nato war exercises.

Ireland is an example which has become known for its UN role. Ireland was one of the few west European countries which did not join Nato at its inception in 1948, despite being very much a western country and a practising Catholic one too, which was unlikely to make it sympathetic to communism. The grounds at the time were that since Nato countries had to recognise each others' borders, membership would amount to accepting partition in the north, and the 1940s' Fine Gael government of Ireland was on a vigorous anti-partition campaign, continually raising the issue at the UN and everywhere, claiming that a part of its own rightful territory was being 'occupied' by Britain. But having stayed outside Nato, sentiment in Ireland began to hanker after a playing a role in the wider world, and by the 1960s it had become settled that Ireland was a keen participant in UN peacekeeping, and there was considerable satisfaction with the fact.

Source: UN Photo/Albert Gonzalez Farran

Some people would say that it is one thing for a small country to seek a wider role through its participation with the UN, but another for a major country like Britain. We reply that that it is precisely the more major powers whose participation is required for a non-trivial advance towards a better world order. It is a question of Britain becoming more in tune with the mass of smaller countries in the world, when it is not obsessing with retaining great power status.

Other criticisms would focus on the deficiencies of the UN, which exist but have to be lived with, as the only international forum whose legitimacy is universally accepted. For the foreseeable future we are stuck with the vetoes of the permanent members of the Security Council, but we have to regard that as an expression of power reality. These major powers have to agree among themselves before they can agree in the UN. But it is only if they can agree that we can advance the role of the UN.

But doesn't all this show that our ideas are impractical, in fact idealistic moonshine? This book has been almost entirely about Russia and the west, but what about China for a start? Can anyone see the present Chinese regime, and almost any future Chinese regime either, agreeing to have the UN so much a more powerful body that it could decide on the status of Taiwan over any Chinese objections? Or insisting that China open up its camps for the Uighurs to international inspection? It may be that we will have to wait until reformists come to power in China, as one day they surely will, and when they do, we must do what we can to ensure the same wrong response does not come from the west for a second time. This is a highly nontrivial point, since at the moment there are plenty who will tell us that the only mistake about Nato enlargement was that we did not do it hard enough. Only a few weeks before the present Ukraine events, Britain, America and Australia signed a new Pacific pact openly aimed at surrounding China. It started farcically by offending the French instead, for not buying a weapon system off them, but in intention it is not exactly a good sign.

Still, you can persist, what about China? And what about all the other quarrels in the world, some among quite powerful countries in their own right, like India and Pakistan? Or the seemingly eternal and insoluble problems of the Middle East?

All these problems will have to be worked through, and are unlikely to disappear for generations yet, but the only alternative is to let them fight it out, and what's more, since them fighting it out is bound to be complicated by outside powers choosing sides and backing rival regimes as part of their own continuing Great Game, continuation of a present situation which sooner or later would be bound to culminate in someone letting off a nuclear weapon. This brings us to multilateral nuclear disarmament.

Multilateral nuclear disarmament

When it comes to the future, the main question in most people's minds is what to do about nuclear weapons. Even the Strangeloves who regard them as the saviour of the world from war admit (usually) that there are problems, most obviously proliferation. You can take the view that so long as it's your country alone (i.e. provided other countries don't do the same as you) they are the ultimate security guarantee, not to mention the weight it lends to your own greatness. But to everyone else it's clear that the only policy which makes sense is nuclear disarmament by international agreement.

This means above all the rediscovery, for the nuclear powers, of Clause 6 of the Non-Proliferation Treaty of the 1960s, towards which they have shown such bad faith. Here is an opportunity for Britain with a reformed foreign and defence policy to take a lead. Just as Britain with the famous 'zeal of a reformed sinner' took the lead in the 19th century in suppressing the Atlantic slave trade, and then was at the front of moves to abolish slavery altogether, Britain can be at the front of moves towards control and reduction of nuclear weapons, and with some eventual goal which makes sense. This goal cannot be complete relegation of nuclear weapons to history, since nuclear weapons cannot be uninvented, but must be some sort of monopoly of ownership by an agreed international body working under international rules.

In the short term the aim should be the passing of proposals which will limit the spread of nuclear weapons, and such proposals must include the nuclear powers' own plans to gradually decrease their stocks, and a commitment to eventual abolition which must be seen as a genuine commitment and not just a brush-off piece of verbiage. But how can we reconcile a long-term goal of abolition by all individual nations with the present situation of nuclear powers who won't move in that direction so long as others won't, and aspirant nuclear powers who will seek to become actual nuclear powers so long as other countries are? How can we even start to move away from this situation?

In the 1990s the American disarmament writer Jonathan Schell suggested so-called 'threshold status' as a feasible medium-term step towards a long-term aim of a world nuclear regime. Threshold status is when a country has the knowledge and skill, and the industrial base necessary, to manufacture nuclear weapons, but refrains from the actuality of doing so for the time being. For political reasons it remains a non-nuclear power, but if some situation was to arise in which it would deem it necessary, it would be able to produce them at short notice. Threshold status is something intermediate between nuclear power status and non-nuclear power status but can also be presented as something that a nuclear power can offer without ceasing to claim the status of a nuclear power.

Japan is often presented as an example of threshold status. It is known to have the means to produce nuclear weapons, and it seems clear that it carefully preserves all knowledge and industrial base necessary to do so if they made the decision. True Japan does not have any immediate adversarial-looking power facing it (though there are intermittent tensions with China in the aftermath of the Second World War, and a small amount of tension with Russia over some islands Russia took at the end of the Second World War), but even countries with quarrels with others, some of whom look as if they are going for nuclear status, might be persuaded to stop at threshold status instead.

Britain could feasibly offer threshold status without actually sacrificing very much at all. It could keep the submarines, and the American missiles to put in them, though it would have to render the warheads inactive, and it would have to be subject to some sort of international inspection that this was the case. No doubt there would be all sorts of secrecy and security objections, but these could be overcome if there was the will. The submarines could even continue patrolling, to keep in exercise, something suggested by the Labour leader in the 2016 election. It was predictably rubbished by his opponents, who sneered at the notion of missile-carrying submarines without the missiles (but then, they would, wouldn't they?), but as a realisation of threshold status it could be offered in disarmament negotiations, unjamming what otherwise seems an insoluble conundrum.

The long-term aim has to be the setting up of an agreed international body to take charge of the remaining nuclear weapons on earth, have robust inspection regimes and enforcement procedures against the occasionally obstinate and bellicose. One of Britain's international roles would be contribution to the international enforcement regime of course. It will be difficult, but there is no other long term survival strategy for humanity.

Envisioning the future

What sort of long-term objective should we be envisioning for Britain and the world? We have spoken of an eventual international authority to supervise and have sole authority over nuclear weapons. But nuclear weapons (and more generally weapons of mass destruction) are not the only problem of the world, though they are the most dramatic and alone make it ridiculous to talk about the world as if they did not exist. Equally ridiculous are those who seem to think, or talk as if they think, Britain would be safer in a world in which every country has nuclear weapons pointing at every other country in perpetuity. Nuclear weapons have to be controlled at an international level, and also the many other problems of an over-armed world with advanced technological weaponry.

But what of the more general issues of the future? After all, the present claim being made is that we are trying to preserve a 'rules-based international order,' and even if this is mainly rhetoric as a denunciation of Putin, it is right enough that that is what we should be aiming for. But in what form exactly? An old-fashioned answer is to call for eventual world government, but we think it must be something less absolute and more involved than that. Anything like a unitary world state, however eventually, would not be acceptable to a majority at the UN either in the Security Council or the General Assembly, especially since it would be dominated by the west. And there are general and objective problems associated with it. Suppose the government of such an entity fell into the hands of extremists like the Nazis or Bolsheviks or even religious extremists? Such regimes occur from time to time and must be reckoned to continue to occur. So far, they have occurred in a few individual countries, and there existed an outside world in which their internally ubiquitous doctrines and state-controlled media did not hold. But suppose there existed no outside world, so that their view of the world and control of everything was unchallenged? This unitary world would either be self perpetuating, or any instability in it would by definition be instability on a world scale.

The post-first world war allies probably got it right – a 'League of Nations' (perhaps a better name for it than United Nations, though the name has stuck by now), for that has become the recognised international body whose obligations every country seems willing to accept at least in theory. The aim is obviously to make the theory eventually become the accepted reality, and Britain should lead towards that goal.

League of Nations Semi-official flag (1939)

Those who consider that we are just talking lily-livered appeasement of the enemies of freedom, law and all we hold dear, should ask themselves what exactly their own vision for the future is. Is it that we will fight the righteous fight against Russia and batter it down into submitting to a western led world order, and after due punishment is allowed to take its diminished place in Nato's sphere of hegemony? And having dealt with Russia, we will then deal with China in the same way? And also, Iran, and anyone else who has challenged western hegemony over the world, or at least caused it trouble, or at least offended us in some way? And all (presumably) without a nuclear or biological weapon being fired off, or at least not landing on us? You have only to think a moment. Wars are started not so much by the self-consciously wicked but by the blinkered self-righteous, and here is the ultimate example.

Conclusion

There is surely no serious alternative to our proposals for the further future. Details aside, this is the direction Britain should take, and it suggests a future for Britain which conservatives as well as left wingers could accept and take pride in. The country that was the greatest in the age of empires can become great again, in the new 21st century form of greatness, in a leading role in a seriously created world community that has developed institutions, procedures and forms of practice that can continue world diversity but control what has to be controlled, which is the darker side of humanity.

Bite-Sized Books

Why not sign up to our mailing list here:

Why not browse our BOOKSHOP?

More about Bite-Sized Books here:

Printed in Great Britain
by Amazon